FOR Rich and Mary,

Barbara Ashmun
April 1996

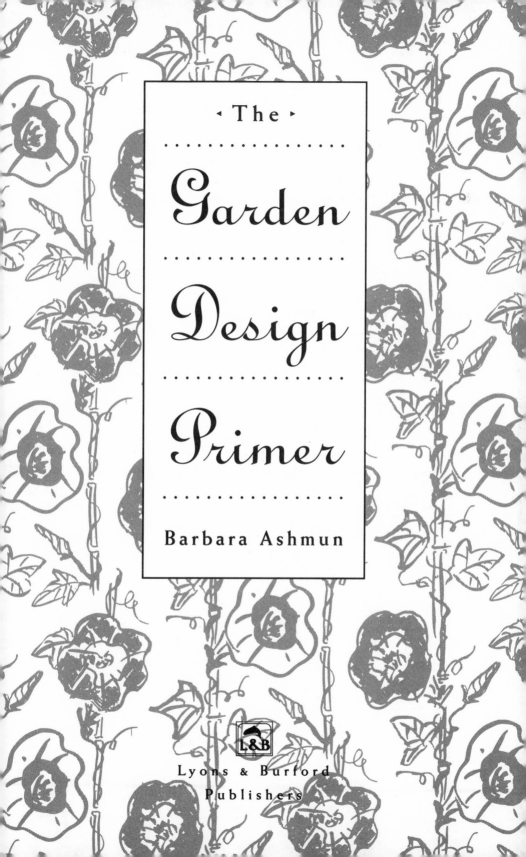

‹ The ›

Garden Design Primer

Barbara Ashmun

L&B

Lyons & Burford
Publishers

Printed in the United States of America
Illustrations by Christine Erikson
Design by Kathy Kikkert

10   9   8   7   6   5   4   3   2   1

Ashmun, Barbara.
The garden design primer / Barbara Ashmun.
p.   cm.
Includes bibliographical references and index.
ISBN 1-55821-257-4 (cloth)
ISBN 1-55821-388-0 (paperback)

1. Gardens—Design. 2. Landscape gardening. I. Title
SB473A735   1993
712—dc20   93-41415
CIP

Contents

. . .

Acknowledgments

· · ·

Whether we know it or not, we transmit the presence of

everyone we have ever known, as though by being in each

other's presence we exchange our cells, pass on some of our life

force, and then go on carrying that other person in our body,

not unlike springtime when certain plants in fields we walk

through attach their seeds in the form of small burrs to

our socks, our pants, our caps, as if to say, "Go on, take

us with you, carry us to root in another place."

"The Long Quiet Highway"

—Natalie Goldberg

· · ·

From childhood on, many teachers guided me on the path to writing this book. I am grateful to my parents, Ben and the late Anne Nemerow, who taught me to value discipline, perseverance, and accomplishment. My sister, Sarita Eisenstark, made my serious childhood world lighter and broader and opened the doors of imagination. My aunt, the late Libby Jaffe, showed me how to have fun and laugh until I cried. She loved me even when I made mistakes.

When I began to garden, my neighbor, the late Frank Curtis, patiently taught me how to spade, plant, prune, and nurture the plants. Herb Orange, my first horticulture teacher, gave me unlimited encouragement and support. Herb said I was capable of anything, and I believed him; he never once offered dire warnings about job prospects. He pushed me forward and accelerated my learning by offering me challenging projects and taking me to see beautiful gardens.

Ray A. McNeilan, Oregon State extension agent, introduced me to many aspects of gardening and to experienced gardeners and growers who took me further. I frequently ran behind perennial nurseryman Ed Wood and expert gardeners Faith MacKaness and David Palmer, frantically photographing and writing down plant names that they rattled off in impeccable botanical Latin.

Three key people helped me move from a career in social work to a life as a gardener and garden designer. When I expressed fears about earning a living, Paul Kleffner asked the right question: "How much is your peace of mind worth?" I sat on the sofa and pondered that one. Pat Sims allowed me to see that my heart and soul needed a creative outlet, and that it was fine to give up social work. And Joe Dubay taught a class called "Life Work Planning" that helped me shift gears and move my life forward.

I am grateful to the many gardeners, growers, and garden designers who welcomed me to study, photograph, and learn from their gardens, especially Jan Waltenmath, Margaret Willoughby, Penny Vogel, Millie Kiggins, Cynthia Woodyard, John and the late Jane Platt, John Borowczak, Michael S. Schultz, Loie Benedict, Stephen Carruthers, John Caine, the late Constance Hansen,

Lorena M. Reid, Al and Dot Rogers, Dulcy Mahar, Elizabeth Marantz, Vern Nelson, Brewster Rogerson, Ruth Kaufman, Sue Thomas, Dorothea Lee, Maurita Smyth, and Lori Delman.

I thank the many clients who trusted me to create new gardens for them, especially Janet Geary, in whose garden I worked with great pleasure for six years. I am grateful to Celia Nemerow, Susan Jones, Bill Grant, Nancy Beaubaire, Pamela Harper, Heidi Yorkshire, Nancy Woods, Martha Wagner, and Mary Stupp-Greer for all their help, encouragement, and advice about creating a book: brand-new territory for me.

I could not have accomplished the writing of a book without the loving support of friends who cheered me on, cooked for me, put up with my ups and downs, and gave me space and time to write. My heartfelt thanks to Dick Van Ingen, Ruth Mackey, Sandy Childress, Donna Freeman, Betty Barker, Anita Morrison, Virginia Plainfield, Paula Hougland, LaVerne Kludsikofsky, and Mary Huey.

To the infinite source of creativity that lives within each of us.

Preface

. . .

I grew up in New York City, where the only gardening I did was on the windowsill of my Manhattan apartment. I remember that the city grit made the windowsill so gray with soot that I finally painted it black. I grew marbled green pothos, striped spider plant, and avocado pits that became miniature trees on that black windowsill.

When I moved to Portland, Oregon in 1972, I might as well have been Alice in Wonderland opening a door to incredible wonder. Purple bearded iris and red oriental poppies thrilled me with their big flowers. Even the freeway plantings of yellow broom and orange-berried firethorn excited me. I was bitten by flower gardening through color, much as finger paints and crayons grabbed me when I was little.

I grew everything I could cram into pots on the small patio of my first apartment in Portland: petunias, marigolds, lobelia, sweet alyssum. I marveled at the colors and fragrances. I was in gardener's kindergarden, in love with primary colors: bright red, yellow, and blue.

The following year I moved to a house on a city lot, all of 50' × 100'. It seemed enormous compared to apartments. Learning about the trees and shrubs on the lot was exciting, but it wasn't long before I began to remove old plants and select new ones that I liked better. I started growing perennials and learning about their flowers and leaves. I couldn't believe that they came back each year, bigger and stronger.

Growing vegetables was another adventure. I was amazed that I could take small seeds, germinate them indoors, plant these seedlings out in the garden, and watch them bear tomatoes and cucumbers that tasted so much better than store-bought. It was all miraculous, this business of tending plants that flowered and fruited. Nothing on earth felt better than working in the garden.

When I had planted every inch of that small city lot, except for a few narrow grass paths, I was in trouble. Arriving home from the nursery with a new plant, I'd have to dig out an old one to make room for the newcomer. It was time to move to a bigger garden with a smaller house.

I now garden on two-thirds of an acre, where I can barely keep up with the weeding, but have enough room to experiment. After seven years of intense gardening, I've nearly filled the available space with beds and borders. Next year I'll begin to refine the existing beds, removing the less desirable plants and reshaping some of the awkwardly formed spaces. I'd like to add a sheltered seating area, and perhaps a small greenhouse and cold frames and . . .

The garden has changed and shaped my life. My first career was in medical social work; and when I worked in a hospital, I noticed that I looked longingly out the windows at the gardeners. I wished I were in their shoes. I lived for evenings in the garden, early mornings in the garden, and eventually lunch hours in the garden.

Sick and dying patients lying in their hospital beds told me their regrets, their unfulfilled dreams. I listened and saw that I'd be in the same place if I didn't do something different—soon. As my discontentment with hospital social work pushed me out, the garden pulled me forward to a new life.

I resigned from my job in 1980, on the first day of spring. I gardened and studied gardening by reading, taking classes, and joining gardening societies. I volunteered for every opportunity to garden that might be a learning experience; the local botanic gardens and nonprofit agencies all needed help. I spent time in nurseries learning about plants. Occasionally I worried about earning a living, but mainly I gardened. I followed my heart.

Soon friends began to ask me to help them with their gardens. A friend suggested that I teach. A landscaper asked me to help him with garden maintenance. I said yes to everything. I took every job until my time was filled up. I hadn't made a five-year plan. The garden had led me gently to a new life.

I discovered that teaching garden classes and consulting with homeowners in their gardens are my favorite kinds of work. A big part of gardening is sharing love for the plants and joining with others to admire and learn more. I love to pass along my knowledge and excitement: when I get a new gardener started, I am overjoyed.

Writing is my next step in sharing my gardening experience, another way to teach and reach out to more new gardeners. The garden has given me so much joy that I want to extend that experience to you. My hope is to give you some guidelines to allow your path in gardening to be smooth and successful. I urge you to make the journey your own and encourage you to experiment and have fun along the way.

Introduction

. . .

When we grasp the concept of metamorphosis in evolving

nature and consciousness, when we meditate upon the forming-

ness of life all about us, we can begin to experience in ourselves

the stages of development. We can grasp the fact that

at any moment what seems most certain to us is an illu-

sion. It is an illusion in that it precedes and presages

a further revelation about ourselves.

—M. C. Richards

Centering in Pottery, Poetry, and the Person

. . .

Most of us begin to garden because we've fallen in love with plants, color, or fragrance. We see an iris saturated with purple, a tomato-red poppy decorated with inky-black blotches, or a fragrant satin-pink rose, a luminous white magnolia, and we are lost. We must have these flowers growing in our own gardens. This can go on for years as we collect plants of many heights, shapes, and in every color of the rainbow, enjoying and loving each individual miracle.

But one day gnawing dissatisfaction begins to set in when we see that there is no flow to this vast assemblage of beauty. This realization might occur after visiting a friend's garden that has been laid out in a pleasing, orderly fashion, or after browsing through a garden book filled with serene color photographs of mature, well-designed gardens. My first such revelation came after seeing a friend's perennial border blooming in shades of pink, blue, and purple. I was so envious! She had no clashing, jarring colors fighting for attention as I did; there was no mustard yellow or screaming orange. It suddenly dawned on me that I, too, could choose color schemes and order over rainbow plantings and chaos. My friend wasn't just lucky, she was selective and purposeful in her planting. First she used her imagination to visualize the colors she enjoyed together; then she went out and shopped for plants. This was exactly the opposite of what I had been doing for years. Could I make this shift?

For many of us, gardening begins with a love of flowers. I fell in love at the age of four. Growing up in a high-rise apartment building in New York City, I didn't get to garden until moving to Oregon in 1972. But at four I was chosen to be a flower girl for my glamorous Aunt Rose's wedding. I so loved the feel and fragrance and color of the rose petals in my small wicker basket that I hardly scattered any petals on the aisle, much to the bride's disappointment. Years later, coming to garden as an adult, it was the same. The color, fragrance, and texture of flowers took my breath away. I would get up early in the morning before work to pry open the buds of oriental poppies, to see and photograph their red crepe-papery petals, marveling at the flower's unfolding.

However, I failed to look up and out at the shapes and heights of trees, shrubs, and structures that give the garden form. My eyes were always at flower level. A visiting friend, looking at the front of my house, started waving her hands around in the air, trying to show me how the house needed framing with plants. She was drawing lines in the air to describe how the trees and shrubs should flow to tie the house to the garden from canopy to understory to ground cover. I tried to look casual and knowing, but in fact I was so surprised my mouth might as well have hung open. I had never considered shapes, lines, or flow to be part of gardening. Doors were beginning to open to new concepts, and I was on my way to learning about design, about planning with purpose. In this book, I shall be taking you through the steps to become your own designer, sharing what friends, teachers, students, and experience have taught me.

Coming to gardening later in life than many others, I worried about jumping in too late until I saw a garden made by a woman in her fifties, and then a garden created by a woman in her seventies. I realized that it is never too late; the trick is to seize the moment, act as if you have forever, and at the same time understand that there is never enough time. Experience every moment that you spend in the garden and use all your senses to observe what is there. Learn to see the colors; smell the fragrances; touch the textures; listen to the birds and wind; soak in the beauty.

Forget the concept of perfection and know that gardening is a process to enjoy, to learn from, and to refine continually. You don't need to master it; rather, become a partner with the elements of nature and the elements of art, aligning yourself with already-existing principles and forces to create something new that is yours for the moment. To what end? Your own pleasure, the pleasure of friends, connection with the earth and seasons, balance, health, a brick in the path of world peace and unity. You will find more purposes and benefits that are yours to discover along the way, and meet wonderful new friends with whom to share the journey.

Understand that gardening is a process that changes as we change and as the world around us changes. Tastes in color, plants, and composition evolve with growing knowledge and observation. Life-style changes create new needs in the design, perhaps for outdoor entertaining spaces or children's play areas. We may have to adjust to climactic changes imposed by the external world and learn to conserve water, or create shelter from wind. As our bodies age, we may move toward raised beds and lower maintenance requirements. Allow room for change and flexibility. The best gardeners are armed with shovel and wheelbarrow and a glint in their eyes, moving things around for an even better garden. There is always a new plant that we must have, and a friend newer to gardening to take the discards. Gardens are a mirror of life, changing, moving, evolving as we grow.

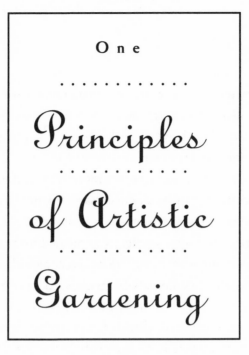

One

· · · · · · · · · · ·

Principles

· · · · · · · · · · ·

of Artistic

· · · · · · · · · · ·

Gardening

Learning the principles of art will help guide you in the process of creating an artistic garden. Once you know these basic ideals, you will recognize their presence in all forms of creativity, whether painting, sculpture, music, or literature. These are universal truths. Now, I doubt seriously that the early artists, musicians, or writers sat down and formulated these principles. It's more likely that when we study beauty in any form and begin to analyze what makes it wonderful, these are the qualities that we can name in words: simplicity, balance, scale, harmony, and unity. Since these are ideals, we aim for them, work toward them, and understand that they come gradually with time and patience.

Simplicity is the result of great refinement and elimination of all that is lumpy, bumpy, and unnecessary. A simple strand of pearls may have an elaborate clasp and complexity of subtle, lustrous color, but there is nothing extraneous to distract from the beauty of the pearls. A ceramic bowl might have a complex glaze and textural detail, yet achieve simplicity by its classical form. Simplicity is a word trying to convey the state of wholeness where the details of the object are small and refined enough to be secondary to the main presence, and in harmony with the whole. A well-made Japanese garden is deceptively simple in that every tree, rock, and body of water is placed purposefully and is vital to the picture. All the clutter, busyness, and unnecessary embellishment is absent. Simplicity is often the last quality achieved in a garden, especially for plant lovers like me. It takes discipline and restraint to remove excessive fussiness and move toward simplicity.

Balance is a bit easier to achieve, although the concept covers a lot of ground. One part of balance considers the different weights of structural masses and plant materials in adjacent parts of the garden. For example, if you look at the front garden of a home as if it were a painting, a large shade tree placed to one side of the entry, creating a substantial canopy, will need an equivalent mass on the other side. You can create it by placing several shrubs there, or possibly a structural element such as an arbor. There is no requirement for symmetry or formality—just for a balancing of weight on opposite sides of the composition.

Another balancing act in the garden occurs between stimulation and tranquillity, between riotous color and quiet, between stretches of flower border and areas of soothing grass or subdued ground cover. Balance between plant materials and empty space, which sets off the plant materials, is also important.

> *Thirty spokes share the wheel's hub;*
> *It is the center hole that makes it useful.*
> *Shape clay into a vessel;*
> *It is the space within that makes it useful.*
> *Cut doors and windows for a room;*
> *It is the holes which make it useful.*
> *Therefore profit comes from what is there;*
> *Usefulness from what is not there.*
> —Lao Tsu

Think about the balance between deciduous plants and evergreen, bearing in mind that evergreens create blocks of green that darken and thicken that garden, while deciduous plants change with the seasons, letting in light when it's darkest, in winter, then going dormant to reveal structural interest. Here the balance is between static evergreens that give a sense of permanence and density, and dynamic deciduous plants that offer seasonal change and a process of metamorphosis. You can achieve interest throughout the year if you pay attention to the balance of seasonal bloom periods. If you choose your plants carefully your garden will offer beauty in spring, summer, and especially in fall and winter, when we most need a lift as the days shorten and light diminishes.

Consider balancing your own purposeful planning and the happy accidents that occur in a garden. The perennial that sows itself in an unplanned place, the fortunate combinations that occur on their own, are all parts of gardening pleasure. There is a happy medium between our deliberate controlling hand and the exuberance of nature and the elements.

Scale is a crucial element in design and contributes to balance. Scale has to do with proportions, or how the sizes and shapes of the house, patios, terraces, beds, borders, and paths relate to each other. A two-story home calls for ample pathways and big trees, with proportionately generous beds. A smaller ranch-style home needs a lower canopy, and paths and beds in more modest dimensions. Begin with the size of the house and property, and design garden features that are in good proportion. It is easier to tell when your scale is incorrect. Your garden will feel imbalanced, cramped, lopsided, disjointed. One of the toughest design problems is a large contemporary house placed on a small, narrow lot, because there is not enough room to plant in proper scale. Correct scale will not be noticed as all will be well and in synch; it is like health, often passing unnoticed until it is absent.

Most new gardeners err on the side of smallness, making paths too narrow and beds too skimpy. Gardening experience teaches us that plants need room to grow, and usually surpass our expectations; people need more room to move in than we estimate. The best gardeners I have met are generous by nature, like good cooks, and lean toward excess with their boundless enthusiasm. I urge you to be bold and generous, and your garden will reward you in equal measure. You will make mistakes no matter how careful you are—there is simply no learning without mistakes— so you might as well enjoy the process with gusto.

Scale has another aspect that is more personal. Some of us like the majestic feeling of large open spaces, with high canopies and vistas that extend outward. Others prefer the intimacy of small enclosed spaces with low canopies. These differences in taste will contribute to your garden style and scale. You may choose to have big, open spaces in some parts of the garden and cozy enclosures tucked away elsewhere. Remember to keep each in scale.

Harmony is the resulting feeling of peacefulness and attunement in a mature, well-planned garden. When you are in harmony with yourself, your mind, heart, and spirit are united and working together in the same direction. Your garden arrives at a state of harmony when the plants join together in a gradual, subtle, easy way. Trees, shrubs, and ground covers blend together as if they have always been there. Paths, fences, and structures belong where they have been placed, and tie together easily with the beds and borders in a natural way.

Harmony is an ideal that we work toward. Here are some guiding pointers. See that shifts in texture, color, line, size, and form are gradual rather than sudden. For example, a magnolia with big bold leaves needs neighboring shrubs with somewhat smaller leaves, perhaps Mexican orange, and a ground cover with even smaller leaves, possibly sweet woodruff, so that a gradual change in texture occurs. The eye receives subtle shifts more easily than abrupt leaps, whether the change is in texture or color. Small transitions from white flushed with pink to light pink to medium rose-pink to deep burgundy create harmony. Juxtaposing light pink and deep burgundy will bring excitement and drama to the garden, but causes the eye to take a big jump from light to dark with nothing to knit the colors together. Think of the garden as a tapestry or a watercolor, and you will begin to understand the image of harmony, or gradual transitions that promote a feeling of peaceful blending.

Unity is similar to harmony and is the end result of all the pieces of the garden jigsaw puzzle fitting together into one united whole. Some of this comes with time and age of a garden as tree canopies mesh together a bit, shrubs join each other to make borders, and perennials weave together to create color compositions. To work toward unity, keep in mind that similarities unite more easily than opposites. If your house is brick, repeat that material in pathways, perhaps varying the pattern for interest. Notice the shape of your roofline and repeat it in the lines of the arbors. If the patio is exposed aggregate, let your stepping-stones be the same. Tie your fencing into your neighbor's with a similar style and material for a continuous look, or soften the differences by covering them with vines. Mute the harsh edges of pavement with overlapping plants. Unite the sky and earth by remembering to create canopy with trees or pergolas, understory of shrubs, and descend to lower perennials and ground covers in a gradual fashion. Repeat enough similarities in the picture that a thread of familiarity runs through to weave it together toward unity.

· RHYTHM, REPETITION, CONTRAST, · AND FOCAL POINTS

To visualize the elements of design, simplicity, balance, scale, harmony, and unity, imagine that these are the five horizontal lines of the musical staff. Plants, wood, stone, water, brick, earth, and sky are the musical notes, and chords are created by harmonizing these notes. Themes are established by creating color schemes or compositions of plants within the garden. Tempo in music finds its garden counterpart in rhythm, flow, and repetition, which are ways to move through garden space. Plants and building materials are repeated at intervals to give a sense of familiarity, evoking an "Ah, there's an old friend again." Colors and groupings of colors may recur, vertical or horizontal lines repeat, setting up a rhythm, a sense of order and predictability. Too much becomes monotonous, too little chaotic; one strives for the balance. Leave room for surprises: the unexpected chord, the transition to a minor key, the variation on a theme. The best gardeners follow their intuition and allow whimsical touches to delight the visitor.

Contrast of color, line, texture, and form is important for drama in the garden, and should be used carefully. You might juxtapose vertical and horizontal lines in fencing or plants to set up strong opposition. Contrasting colors such as purple and yellow or blue and orange set up an electric field and grab your attention. Place a roundheaded tree behind a shelflike slab of dwarf conifer and you create a dynamic tension between opposing shapes. As contrast creates excitement, there is room for some of it, but too much will dispel unity, harmony, and simplicity, leaving the viewer restless and overstimulated. How much is enough? How much pepper do you like in your food?

Focal points can be thought about similarly. Too many make for a busy garden, but a few give a sense of landing and restfulness. Our eyes are working overtime to take in all the color, texture, line, and form; a brief respite is welcome. A bench, an urn, a birdbath, a piece of sculpture, a sundial, a pot or large rock; any stationary object of interest can create a focal point. Proper placement is important. The viewer should be subtly led to the focal point; perhaps down a curved path, or through an inviting arch that frames the picture. A birdbath or sundial within an island bed or border can anchor a floating sea of perennials and give the viewer a moment of rest from color and movement. A focal point serves much like a sorbet between courses. Antique urns and aged stonework can also create a feeling of permanence, suggesting solidity and timelessness. A carefully chosen and artistically placed stone in a Japanese garden can encourage contemplation. Even a small water basin brings reflections and birds. Benches are pretty and remind us how pleasant it will be someday to actually sit down and look.

Two

Choosing
a Theme

With so many possibilities to choose from, it helps to have a theme in planning a garden; not as a hard-and-fast rule to stick to, but as a guiding light. There are many purposes for a garden, and I encourage you to think about what you want. Here are some choices.

My claim to fame as a garden designer is creating year-round color, and that was the theme I began with. At first I searched for plants with long bloom periods that began to flower in early winter and continued into spring. I included plants that flowered in spring and summer and made an extra effort to find fall-blooming plants that lasted well into November. I made a point of looking for plants that had seed pods, fruit, berries, and beautiful bark to add interest in fall and winter. Although year-round color was the original theme, creating color combinations soon became a second concern. I was not satisfied with simply having a sequence of bloom, I wanted smashing color compositions during all seasons. Thus began a series of experiments with color and texture to achieve satisfying combinations for every season, and my theme now is a living laboratory of plant compositions. Always eager to try new plants and unusual combinations, I have a garden that is changing constantly.

My friend Ruth Mackey chose fragrance as her theme. She has a keen nose and is able to distinguish between sweet, spicy, and fruity scents, where I am lucky to pick up any fragrance at all. With a finely tuned appreciation for perfume and a small garden, she has chosen this quality to maximize her garden pleasure and also help narrow down the plant choices from the overwhelming array available in the Pacific Northwest. Her roses, lilies, and most of her perennials and annuals must be scented, with only a few exceptions where love of color overruled the theme.

A fellow designer decided to create an organic, edible landscape and make that his theme. He grows a wide variety of fruits, grows vegetables in raised beds, raises chickens for eggs and manure, and composts regularly to improve his soil. A pergola loaded with kiwi fruit, apples trained to a Belgian fence and an oblique cordon add interesting structural ornamentation while producing practical crops. Some perennials, annuals, and herbs are grown for color, but the priority is food production and organic horticulture. His garden is not only a source of personal accomplishment, but a demonstration and teaching tool that is shared with the larger community. There is nothing as persuasive as sharing a taste of sun-ripened fig; I planted a fig tree shortly after visiting Vern's garden.

For more private souls, the garden is a place for retreat, meditation, tranquillity. The importance of visual screening with fences, walls, trees, hedges, or shrub borders will take priority in planning. Noise reduction might be necessary as well if nearby traffic or neighbors intrude on privacy. This is sometimes helped by circulating water that provides a steadier, hypnotic sound, muffling other noises, or very thick walls. Simplicity of plant materials, cool and pastel colors—perhaps a white garden, expanses of soothing green, emphasis on texture and form rather than color, will add to a climate of calm. Places to sit and meditate, a water feature to focus on, or wind chimes to set a mood, may be considered. A garden I once visited had a beautiful marble sculpture of Kuan Yin, another had a bronze Buddha, each a reminder of spiritual ideals we aim toward in meditation. A favorite place in my garden is a bench under the grape arbor, where I can sit and look out at a sculpture of a sleeping gardener. A small break watching him reminds me to rest occasionally, too.

The garden as an outdoor living space is another theme to consider. Practical features determine the plan: play areas for children, sports courts for adults, places to barbecue, swim, sit and eat, or simply lounge about. This kind of landscape calls for tough plants that can withstand straying balls and active children, and level surfaces suitable for chairs and tables. Try to keep leaf fall and fruit drop to a minimum near pools, ponds, and patios. Usually this life-style requires either low-maintenance plants or a garden service to take care of the grounds, as the homeowner is more interested in sports, entertaining, and relaxing than in weeding and pruning. It's better to acknowledge these priorities and plan accordingly than try to do it all and feel overwhelmed. Planting trees and shrubs that are lower maintenance than perennials, limiting the amount of high-maintenance turf, and choosing easy-care ground covers and bulbs instead of demanding flower beds, will help reduce the work. Well-designed structural elements such as patios, pergolas, walls, fences, pools, and trelliswork are especially important in this kind of garden where the landscape architecture will probably have a stronger impact than the plants.

Many of my clients enjoy cutting flowers from the garden for arranging indoors, and this passion can become a theme. When we plan the garden, we are careful to select trees, shrubs, perennials, bulbs, and annuals that are suitable for cutting. A screening hedge of lilacs will be preferred over photinia, shrub roses will be selected instead of shrub juniper, and lily of the valley will cover shady ground instead of periwinkle (*Vinca minor*). Choices will include shrubs with good leaves for filling in flower arrangements (evergreen huckleberry, Mexican orange), plants with berries for winter bouquets (cotoneaster, beautyberry) and interesting branching patterns for the framework of flower arrangements (corkscrew willow). Favorite colors in the house will be noted as flowers will be brought inside and will have to coordinate with interior design. Flowers for drying, such as hydrangea, astilbe, artemisia, lavender, sea holly, yarrow, and seed pods for drying, such as love-in-a-mist (*Nigella damascena*), Siberian iris, opium poppy and flowering onion (*allium*) might be considered, too. Lovers of potpourri will want to include lemon verbena, lavender, rosemary, scented geraniums, and fragrant roses in their gardens.

There may be one group of plants that you are especially devoted to, and that will give you your theme. If you raise roses for showing, you will probably plan a rose garden, with raised beds enriched with compost, designed for growing the modern hybrid roses well. People who love climbing roses will benefit from attractively designed trellises, pergolas, or arches to support them. Lovers of herbs may be inclined to concentrate on herbal plantings, most of which require a well-drained soil, and lend themselves to a dry garden with a Mediterranean look. Knot gardens might be designed to display a collection of herbs and give them an elegant structure to simultaneously set off and contain their opulent growth habits.

Tree fanciers have been known to create an arboretum for their garden. Those most interested in native plants might begin by planning a garden that blends in well with the already-existing landscape. A concentration of native plants would be selected first.

Then there are gardeners who love to collect, grow, and propagate every possible plant, for whom the process of experimenting is pure joy. A greenhouse, potting shed, and cold frames might be central to such a garden and integrated into the design, rather than hidden in the back forty. Designed with both beauty and function in mind, these work spaces can do double duty and add attractive structural elements to the garden.

Occasionally several neighbors will join forces and link their gardens together. This gives each of them a feeling of spaciousness and continuity as one garden flows into the next, instead of being chopped artificially into smaller pieces by hedges, walls, and fences. One such design that I've seen was parklike in its woodland setting, with large Douglas firs, a shrubby understory, and a uniting ribbon of grass that flowed from garden to garden. Of course this takes a group of neighbors compatible enough to agree on a style that unites their diversity, and who like each other well enough to share space.

Attracting birds to the garden calls for plants with edible berries, dense shrubs and trees for nesting and shelter, and drinking places safe from marauding cats. A garden for the birds as its theme would feature feeders, birdhouses, and birdbaths with quiet places for people to sit and enjoy watching them. View windows or window seats in the house could be designed for looking out. Even though I didn't plan it, preexisting fruit trees, grapevines, and hawthorn trees draw masses of birds to my garden, and they are so delightful that I put up with the twiggy, thorny hawthorns for their sake.

For gardeners who are away during the day and are likely to spend evenings in the garden, consideration should be given to maximize evening enjoyment. Night lighting to illuminate the garden, plants such as *Nicotiana sylvestris* and old-fashioned strains of nicotiana that are fragrant at night, and white as well as pale flowers that show up well in the dark, would all help. Bat houses are gaining vogue for insect control, and certainly a night garden should have one. A woman I know designed a moon garden and filled it with white and off-white flowers: peonies, roses, lilies, bellflowers, delphinium, dahlias, cosmos and feverfew. Silver-foliage plants embellished the white, adding mysterious elegance by moonlight.

Painters often create gardens to paint, cooks make gardens to harvest, romantics garden to create atmosphere, while others simply love to dig and get their fingers in the dirt. For some the garden is to look at, for others to live in, for some to tend, and for others to share. Knowing who you are and what you want from your garden will help you choose your theme.

> *Style is a matter of taste, design a matter of principles.*
> —Thomas Church
> *Gardens Are for People*

· FINDING YOUR STYLE ·

There are two main directions to think about when considering garden style: approaching nature and approaching art. The most natural landscapes are the woodlands, meadows, lakes, ponds, streams, oceanside, mountains, plains, deserts, and rolling hills that we begin with before putting a shovel into the ground. The more closely we imitate these aspects of original landscape, the more natural our gardens will be. Nature's lines are more often irregular with rough edges, and more curvilinear than angular. Features are more likely to be asymmetrical. The more we stylize natural landscape elements by making the lines more regular, definite, and angular, by arranging shapes more symmetrically, the more artful our gardens become and the more formal in design.

Reading about the development of garden style and traveling to other cultures to observe these differences is useful. Even more constructive is studying your own unique garden and the lay of the land. Although human nature often perversely wishes to clear the slate and create with a controlling hand, it's better to capitalize on naturally occurring hills, creeks, ponds, banks, bogs, and woodland, than to force a garden style onto a site that cannot accommodate it. Working with the existing site will make your life easier and harmonize better with the bigger picture, the neighborhood and the surrounding landscape. Don't let this be said of you:

> *The Casa Mia . . . had been built . . . by someone who*
> *had cherished the dream of a villa in Spain and had had*
> *to settle for the next best thing. Its Moorish arches and*
> *wrought iron embellishments looked as out of place in*
> *this very English setting as a tart at a vicar's tea party.*
> —Dorothy Simpson
> *Suspicious Death*

Suppose that your original site is woodland, shady, with a canopy of oak and fir, an understory of shrubby hemlock and vine maple, and a floor of assorted ferns and ground cover. Having always dreamt of living in a Mediterannean villa, you clear the site and start over again, designing a garden with terraces and silver plants. Going to great expense and shifting tons of earth and stone will accomplish this, but how will this design fit into the natural site? You could more easily find a site that better fits your dream, or work with a vision that better fits your site.

How do you summon up a vision? Use your memories as guides. Remember what it's like to walk in the woods and suddenly come upon a waterfall or creek. In your mind's eye, see again the shady woodland trail you walked and the sudden delightful surprise when you entered a sunny meadow filled with wildflowers.

Visit beautiful natural and landscaped woodland gardens and let the images sink into your subconscious creative mind so that you can recall them selectively later on. When I design a new garden, I summon up images of gardens, trails, and scenes that I've seen in the past twenty years to use as inspiration for new compositions. Just as a rich vocabulary will contribute to finer prose, a larger palette of beautiful images will help construct a finer garden design.

Besides looking to the natural landscape to guide you in defining your style, look to yourself, your style of dress, the way you decorate your home, the surroundings that please you. Are you formal, tidy, organized, and inclined to have a place for everything and keep everything in its place? Or are you more casual, able to tolerate or even embrace clutter, profusion, informality, and natural abandon? Do you like tailored understated clothes or more exotic feathers? Do you prefer impressionist paintings, abstract geometric contemporary canvases, or formal portraits? Are you happier on a woodland trail, on top of a mountain, or in a flowering meadow? Are you more at home in the city or country, or somewhere suburban in between? Translating preferences like these to your choices for garden design will help you find your style.

· BECOMING MORE CREATIVE ·

Individual creativity is perhaps the most important and most elusive prerequisite for satisfying garden design. Creativity is inherent in every one of us. As children we all knew how to create with abandon and joy, painting, coloring, making up games, songs, fantasies. As adults we dream every night, our subconscious mind freely creating grand productions in Technicolor. How do we unlock the door to that wonderful place in conscious daylight?

Picture the mind as a great mansion full of rooms. For much

of the day, we are occupied in the office room with ringing phones, coffee smell, talking words. We are in the freeway room filled with thundering cars and blaring radios, in the "please other" room or the "find the right answer" room, the "make money" room. Our minds are bombarded with other people's demands and opinions. Meanwhile the creative room is way in the back of the house, waiting for us to enter. It's quiet there and light and airy and empty, with time and space to be and dream and create.

There are many paths to get there. The obvious first step is to get out of those other rooms! Make a time and a place that is set aside for you to create.

Like cleaning a blackboard, we need to erase the clutter, to make a clean slate before the new images will appear. To give the mind a clear focus, any concentrated activity will do. The hectic mind needs a job to quiet it down. Raking leaves, weeding, cleaning off a desk, singing in harmony, pruning.

In my own garden, weeding is a good way to open the door to creativity. On my hands and knees, as I weed, the repetitive rhythmic pulling of grass, troweling out dandelions, clearing out old leaves, soothes my mind; and soon I have entered a whole new world of leaves, weeds, crumbly earth, slimy slugs, fragile seedlings. As my thoughts and senses are filled with this company of tiny creatures, there is no room left for the worries of everyday life. I become almost part of the garden. Then I can begin to work with it as an insider, with more sensitivity to the textures and colors, with more awareness of how plants fit together and how beds flow from one to the next. I'm no longer a person using a shovel to dig—the shovel and I and the earth are working together, and the process of planting is easy and fluid.

Just as with swimming or dancing, our first ventures in creative design may be awkward and slow. When I first began gardening, I went outside with my *Western Garden Book*, a yardstick, and trepidation in my heart. Spacing, depth of planting, and growth habits were such mysteries to me. Inevitably I would knock on my eighty-year-old neighbor's door and admit that I needed help. My embarrassed despair was short-lived; Frank loved the job of rescuing a gardener in distress. Experienced gardeners are usually as willing to share their successes as skilled cooks are reluctant to. Sometimes a guiding hand can get us unstuck and onto the creative path. Frank would tell me stories of his early adventures in gardening, and I realized with relief that once he was a novice, too. If he could learn, so could I. None of us is born knowing it all.

Sometimes it helps to get inspiration and guidance from books written by gardeners who are ahead of us. For the very visual, photographs are more important than text. I find it comforting to know that there are so many writers, designers, and gardeners who have each found a unique way to create their own vision.

You can't force the creative process any more than you can pry open a flower or change your personality overnight. Sometimes the trick is to start, without any preliminary great ideas. Just one plant can be a jumping-off place. A client had to have *Crambe cordifolia* in her garden, and that became the starting point, with other plants chosen to accompany it, and additional plants enhancing those companions, and so forth.

A favorite color can be a place to start. I could tell the minute we entered her kitchen that one of my clients was in love with cornflower blue and white. We began her border design with those colors in mind. Another client loved pink and blue, while her husband was mad about red and yellow. Thus began the challenge of finding places for both schemes with some spatial separation to prevent them from defeating each other's beauty. Fortunately, their garden is big enough to satisfy both individuals' tastes. In a smaller garden, such differences can be worked out by planning a pink-and-blue spring garden, followed by a red-and-yellow summer color scheme.

Sometimes convenience tells you where to begin. In my present garden, an old compost pile full of lovely soil invited me to begin a bed there. By rearranging the shape a bit, I was able to turn it into a rectangular border that served as a screen between the near and far back yards, the latter being a weedy meadow that I preferred to ignore for a while. Necessity told me where to garden next. A bare square of earth in the middle of the lawn was left after the former owner's trailer home was moved off the property. Rather than seed it with more grass, I expanded it into a circle and designed an island bed for summer-flowering perennials. I liked it so well that I planted two more island beds to join the first in subsequent years; the grouping of three circles that repeat in form but vary in color scheme gives the garden both diversity and unity.

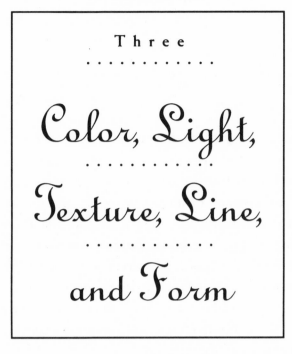

Three
· · · · · · · · · · ·

Color, Light,

· · · · · · · · · · ·

Texture, Line,

· · · · · · · · · · ·

and Form

Only those who love color are admitted to its beauty

and immanent presence. It affords utility to all,

but unveils its deepest mysteries only to its devotees.

—*Johannes Itten*

The Elements of Color

· · ·

· COLOR AND LIGHT ·

Color is the most complex and fascinating aspect of garden design. Entire books have been written about color, so I offer my thoughts as well as a reading list to encourage you to go further. Your best resources, however, are your own eyes. Learning to see

25

the nuances of color and noticing how you respond to color will best teach you how to create a garden that satisfies you.

Although the color wheel commonly used to describe pigment shows only six colors, hundreds of shades, tints, and blends of these hues are actually seen in flowers and leaves. We have words that attempt to define these colors; but, like music, our translations into language are inexact. When you consider how artists over the centuries have used these same colors in so many diverse ways, you will understand how gardeners using the same plant palettes can also bring forth millions of wonderful compositions. We can start by studying other gardeners' creations, but the more we observe and experiment, the more original we can become.

The color of plants, flowers, and garden structures is different from color in painting or other art forms because of the influence of light in the landscape. Not only does the time of day and the corresponding shift of illumination affect color, but there are also weather changes, climatic differences, and seasonal changes to consider. Garden color seen in soft early-morning light is different from the color in midday glare, or the color in early evening's heavenly light. Monet's famous paintings of his garden at Giverny show these changes, with the same garden scene shown at different hours of the day. Overcast skies and damp weather allow garden color to sparkle, while strong sunlight can bleach out a garden's brightness. This is why garden photographers shoot early in the morning or late in the day and welcome an overcast sky. Spring, summer, fall, and winter light vary tremendously, too, and alter garden color. This is in part why the strong deep oranges, reds, and yellows so welcome in fall may seem too jarring in midsummer.

Textural differences in plant material affect color as much as hue. Think of the difference between a leathery green magnolia leaf, the velvety green of moss, and the glossy lacquered green of *Fatsia japonica*. These color variations are created by a combination of leaf thickness, waxiness, smoothness, hairiness, and the resulting light reflectiveness, translucency, or opacity.

· EMOTIONAL RESPONSE TO COLOR ·

The deepest and truest secrets of color effect

are, I know, invisible even to the eye, and

are beheld by the heart alone.

—*Johannes Itten*

The Elements of Color

We all respond emotionally to color, but the same colors can evoke different feelings from one individual to the next. When I teach garden design, I ask my students to describe how each color affects them, and the answers are as different as day and night. For red: warm, exciting, irritating, dominating, wonderful, terrible, fiery, enlivening; for yellow: cheerful, nauseating, powerful, happy; for blue: depressing, uplifting, soothing, cooling, exciting; for white: purifying, spiritual, boring, glaring, unifying, peaceful—and so on. The key point is to ask yourself how these colors make *you* feel. Choose colors that please *you*, and forget the rest. The garden is the place where you can create a world for yourself.

· UNDERSTANDING THE COLOR WHEEL: · HUE, VALUE, INTENSITY

The color wheel is a circle divided into six sectors: red, orange, yellow, green, blue, and violet. These are the basic hues, or colors. Three of these—red, yellow, and blue—are primary colors. Mix these and you will get secondary colors: red and yellow produce orange, yellow and blue produce green, and blue and red produce violet.

Beside the actual hue, color has two other dimensions; value and intensity. A color's value tells you how light or dark it is. Lighter versions of a color are called tints; darker forms are called shades. Sky blue is a tint of blue; navy blue a shade. Intensity describes the saturation of a color, or how bright or pure it is. The more brilliant a color, the higher its intensity; the muddier or more muted it is, the less intense. Delphiniums and cornflowers are intensely blue, as opposed to the muted blue of sea holly (*Eryngium maritimum*) or Stokes' aster (*Stokesia laevis*).

The different colors are more or less intense when compared to each other. To my eye, white is the most intense, leaping out of a bed or border to grab my attention first. Next in intensity is yellow, then orange, then red, then green, blue, and violet. In "The Elements of Color," Johannes Itten formulates the theory that the force of a color equals its brilliance—or intensity—multiplied by its extent (how large an area it covers). This bears remembering and helps us understand why a little bit of a brilliant color goes a long way.

· WARM VERSUS COOL COLORS ·

Red, orange, and yellow are warm colors that jump out to greet you. The next time you're in a crowded room, look around and you'll notice that red, orange, and yellow clothes will catch your eye much faster than blue, green, or violet. Because the warm colors are bright and intense, they give the impression of being closer to you than they actually are. This makes the garden seem smaller—also more exuberant and exciting.

Green, blue, and violet are cooler colors and create a more soothing, restful mood. These colors tend to recede into the distance, helping the small garden appear bigger. Because these colors have less light in them, they are harder to spot, especially in shade, where they tend to disappear into the shadows. They are better seen and appreciated where it is sunny.

If you compare these colors to personalities, the warm colors are like friendly, outgoing people. They're exciting, stimulating; they make their presence known. The cool colors are like quieter people who stay more in the background and give you lots of room to relax. Of course, warm, exciting colors can tire your eyes after a while, just as outgoing people can bowl you over. And the cooler colors can leave you a bit chilled, just like more remote people.

The warm reds, oranges, and yellows are powerful colors; it takes courage and skill to combine them artfully. Vita Sackville-West filled her cottage garden at Sissinghurst with these sunny colors, using orange and yellow columbines, red snapdragons, pokers, and dahlias, yellow yarrows, fennel, mullein, and orange wallflowers. The trick is using a high proportion of green leaves, and paler yellows and oranges, with smaller touches of vibrant red, strong yellow, and bright orange. The brilliant, intense colors are for emphasis, while their lighter-colored relatives serve to blend and unify the picture.

Understand that you can have just so many stars standing out in the garden—those are the strong touches of red, orange, and bright yellow. Around them are the supporting cast of green leaves, light yellow, and creamy orange.

Balancing vertical, horizontal, and rounded flower forms also helps. The vertical lines of yellow foxtail lily (*Eremurus*) contrasting with the rounded red Maltese cross flowers (*Lychnis chalcedonica*) and the pale yellow plates of yarrow (*Achillea* × *taygelea*) contributed to the beauty of a red-and-yellow color scheme at Sissinghurst. The amount of red was small compared to the profusion of yellow and green. Because red is powerful, a little bit is enough.

· THE PALETTE ·

Some comments about color will get you started in making your own personal observations. The more precise your perceptions, the more artful will be your use of color in creating successful combinations.

· Red ·

"Red" is a small word that covers a huge range of color. If you visualize tomatoes, radishes, burgundy wines, velvet curtains, fire engines, and strawberries you will realize how many reds there are. The main difference is whether the red is clear and true, which is rare in the garden, or mixed with blue or yellow. Reds mixed with blue will combine better with other blues, purples, and blue-greens, while reds mixed with yellow are happier with yellow-based orange, browns, and yellow-greens.

Pink, which is red mixed with white, is as variable as red. Pinks that have some yellow in them have names like salmon, apricot, and peach. They look smashing with burgundy foliage beside them and marry well with blue and purple. Salmon and light yellow are good companions, but a strong yellow will drown out the more subtle salmon.

Pinks with blue in them are on their way to being lavender. I like these lavender-pinks with dark blue and purple, creamy white, and pure white. I don't like them near yellow.

Sometimes you can place five or six shades of pink together, and your eye will blend them together, perceiving them harmoniously. A mixed nursery flat of sweet william or astilbe is a good example of that blending.

There is a painter's trick that takes two clashing colors and mixes a few drops of one in the other and vice versa to make two more compatible colors—for example, a few drops of green in a neighboring blue and a few drops of blue in the green. This technique can be done in the garden by taking two plants with clashing colors and finding a third plant that has both colors in it to bind together the clashers. For example, some of the bicolor tulips that contain orange and red can help unite the orange oriental poppies and the red peonies that bloom at the same time. Sometimes red, red-orange, orange, and pinkish red can be joined happily with gay abandon, but this design scheme is not to everyone's taste. It seems to work well in a mix of zinnias, dahlias, or snapdragons; perhaps because the flowers are big, bold, and of equal value.

Two other ways to harmonize clashing blue-reds and orange-reds are to introduce gray foliage or blue flowers, either of which will cool down the fighting fires. Some gardeners use white as a neutralizer, but I find it only draws more attention to the war as white jumps out to jar the eye. Blending, instead of contrasting, is the better strategy in achieving harmony.

• Orange •

Orange offends more gardeners than any other color, yet, used skillfully, it can add lots of life to a garden. At its most intense it can be fluorescent, as in 'Tropicana roses' or California poppies, and in such cases it needs to stand on its own with green foliage to set it off. Toned down a bit, when the flowers are smaller, as in geum, or arranged along the stem in a way that makes the orange less vibrant, as in *Euphorbia griffithii* 'Fireglow,' orange is greatly enhanced by shades of yellow and bronzy-brown. A winning combination in my garden uses *Euphorbia griffithii* 'Fireglow' and orange *Trollius chinensis* accompanied by bronze fennel and golden loosestrife. Orange and purple complement each other, as do orange and blue. Try orange Peruvian lily (*Alstroemeria aurantiaca*) and 'Midnight Blue' beardtongue (*Penstemen*) or bright orange 'Henfield Brilliant' rockrose (*Helianthemum*) with baby-blue forget-me-not (*Myosotis sylvatica*) or love-in-a-mist (*Nigella damascena*). I remember delighting in a fiery planting of orange butterfly weed (*Asclepias tuberosa*) backed by the soothing green of bird's-nest spruce.

Light orange, the color of apricots, is more popular than bright tangerine, evidenced by the growing enthusiasm for such roses as 'Just Joey,' 'Perdita,' 'Tamora,' 'The Yeoman,' and 'Westerland.' When pale orange approaches soft pink we get the lovely shades of 'Apricot Beauty' tulips. Roses described as pink or apricot blends, such as 'Tournament of Roses,' 'Touch of Class,' 'Sheer Elegance,' 'Royal Sunset,' 'Sea Pearl,' 'Frohsinn,' and 'Cathedral,' flower in delicious colors somewhere between pink and orange. They may be enhanced beautifully by the blue of pansies or the blue-violet of lavender or catmint (*Nepeta mussinii*).

· *Yellow* ·

There is more yellow in the garden than any other bloom color, from the earliest light yellow of winter's cornelian cherry (*Cornus mas*) to the latest honey-yellow chrysanthemums of fall. Pale creamy yellow of cream scabious (*Scabiosa ochroleuca*) with its hazy sea of small flowers throughout the summer is easier to combine with other colors than the brassy deep yellow of Coronation Gold yarrow. There is butter yellow, mustard yellow, banana-peel yellow.

A large sweep of yellow marigolds or 'Golden Splendor' lilies with bold flowers creating big color blocks is a very different presentation than the light suggestion of yellow from a diaphanous meadow rue (*Thalictrum speciosissimum*). Small-flowered cornelian cherry in winter light is much subtler than thick-flowering golden chain tree in springtime. Color, intensity, value, flower size, and arrangement on the plant as well as season of bloom all contribute to the impact of color.

Most people like yellow, but some find it too strong for their taste unless it is pastel. There is certainly room for all the ranges of yellow; as there are so many yellow flowers to choose from, the danger lies in overdoing it.

I like yellow best with blue and purple, also combined with red and orange. Some find yellow and white together clean and refreshing, although I must admit they're not my cup of tea.

· *Green* ·

The omnipresence of green is central to the garden's color scheme, since leaves and grass contribute large areas of this color. One word—green—can actually mean the pale yellow-green of new leaves, the bright yellow-green of moss, the dark blackish green of yew, the bluish green of rue, the grayish green of lavender.

So when we speak of a red-and-yellow color scheme, we must remember to include green, the perennial silent partner. And if we are especially sensitive to color, it's best to use greens verging toward yellow with yellow-based color schemes, including orange, brown, and red-orange. Similarly, use greens with blue or gray tints with color schemes that include blues, blue-reds, and violets.

Green also acts as a restful foil to exciting flower color. That's why I keep my lawn, despite complaining about mowing. Expanses of fresh green grass set off the vibrant beds and borders and give the eye a restful break from stronger colors.

Garden greens vary in their constancy as well as their color. Deciduous trees and shrubs leaf out light green, darken with summer, and often turn red, yellow or brown in the fall before disappearing for winter to leave branching structure visible. Most needle and broadleaf evergreens keep their color year-round. Changes are minimal: lighter color of new growth in spring, and cone or berry set in fall. Branching forms are not revealed naturally, and these plants present denser forms, giving more bulk to the garden.

· Blue ·

The true blue of cornflowers is a welcome rarity in the garden. Some gentians, irises, delphiniums, and speedwells come close to true blue, but more often floral blues are mixed with violet or purple. People who prefer the pure true blue of lapis lazuli will have to hunt for its garden equivalent. Most of us happily accept the range of blue-violet, blue-purple, light sky-blue and dark navy-blue, enjoying the variations on a theme.

Blue works well with most other colors. With its complement—or opposite on the color wheel—orange, it sets up an exciting electricity. Blue and red enrich each other; for a touch of luxury, add some purple nearby. Blue and pink, which is a tint of red, are equally successful, and are enriched by a touch of purple or burgundy. Blue and yellow are very popular together, often enhanced with touches of white, gray foliage, and perhaps a bit of red or orange for a little excitement.

I especially like blue to help blend colors that clash. In spring a carpet of forget-me-not helps ameliorate the war between red-orange oriental poppies and blue-red peonies that insist on blooming at the same time. In summer an edging of lavender or catmint frames the rose beds filled with flowers in shades of pink, red, magenta, and apricot. The blue-violet edge suggests unity in spite of the disparity of colors in the roses and flatters all these different hues.

Blue brings the sky into the garden. Its shades and tints please most people. And its horticultural rarity challenges the grower to produce a blue rose, a blue tulip, and bluer spruces.

· Violet, Hot Pink ·

Violet sits between red and blue on the color wheel and includes shades and tints as diverse as eggplant purple, electric hot-pink, mauve or muted pinkish violet, and maroon. The shades approaching purple and maroon look rich with light pink, light blue, or light creamy yellow.

Mauves are trickier, as they can clash with some pinks and look washed out with light blue. Mauve goes well with creamy yellow, ivory white, medium or deep blue, or purple. Silver and blue-green foliage enliven mauve.

The electric hot-pink of moss campion (*Lychnis coronaria*) and bloody cranesbill (*Geranium sanguineum*) are exciting and challenging to combine because of their intensity. Accompanied by gray, deep green or blue-green foliage, they sparkle. Pale, medium, or deep blue set magenta off nicely; purple is enriching. A memorable combination in an English garden placed magenta Armenian geranium (*Geranium psilostemon*) between the burgundy rose 'Roserie de L'Haye' and the lavender-blue spikes of Siberian catmint (*Nepeta sibirica*). The rich green crinkled foliage of this rugosa rose enhanced the cranesbill's magenta flowers as much as the accompanying bloom colors.

· *White* ·

White used in broad masses has dignity and serene beauty, but spotted all about the garden is simply a stirrer up of factions, setting the flowers against one another instead of drawing them into happy relationship.

—Louise Beebe Wilder
Colour in my Garden

White produces the most light and grabs the most attention. This is especially true of the chalk-white flowers of Mt. Fuji summer phlox that dominates the August perennial border, and the bright white evergreen candytuft (*Iberis sempervirens*) that blazes from every rock garden in spring. Pure white is at its best in the shade garden, where its brightness is welcome. It is most effective used alone with shades of green foliage, and enhanced by green foliage variegated with white. A carpet of white-flowering sweet woodruff or snowdrop anemone (*Anemone sylvestris*) is refreshing in a spring woodland garden. A favorite composition in a garden I know has white martagon lilies rising elegantly through a green carpet of bishop's hat (*Epimedium*).

Fortunately there are many off-whites, and whites flushed with pink, yellow, blue and green, to work with. These near-whites blend more harmoniously with their neighbors. The flowers of Korean dogwood (*Cornus kousa*) and evergreen magnolia are closer to ivory, slightly tinted with yellow. The white flowers of masterwort (*Astrantia major*), loved for its fragrance and long summer-bloom period, are often flushed with pink. Many of the white-flowering lilies and daisies have yellow anthers, which warm up the white.

There is nothing equal to white in the garden for a feeling of purity, spirituality, or refreshing coolness. Gardeners seem to appreciate white more with their own deepening experience. There seems to be a developmental progression, with new gardeners drawn to primary colors, then advancing toward pastels and deeper shades for accent, and ultimately appreciating white, texture, and form.

· FOLIAGE COLOR ·

As a new gardener, I was so caught up in the excitement of flowers that leaves were the last thing on my mind—until the day that I saw the bold, rounded wine-colored leaves of *Ligularia* 'Othello.' That was the beginning of my awareness of how much color in the garden comes from foliage: green, gray, gold, silver, red, chocolate. Variegated leaves offer stripes, speckles, and flecks of white, yellow, cream, silver, and even pink.

Leaves provide even longer-lasting color than flowers. Some of the showiest leaves are purple, wine, and coppery-brown, and can be used as dramatic foils. Royal purple smoke tree with euca-lyptuslike leaves gathers many compliments as it stands out sharply against the north side of my blue-gray house. The breath-takingly beautiful River's purple beech makes a dramatic specimen tree in a garden big enough to show it off. In smaller places, 'Palace Purple' coral bells (*Heuchera* 'Palace Purple') is a lovely ac-cent for the shade garden, with leaves varying from coppery brown to rich maroon. These purple-to-wine tones are nicely ac-companied by green, blue-green, gray, silver, pink, orange, pale orange, creamy yellow or blue—it's really hard to go wrong.

Blue-green foliage is soothing and refreshing, especially in the heat of summer. Blue spruce trees—standard, dwarf, or weep-ing—can grace the winter garden and carry the color throughout the year. White fir (*Abies concolor*), with its blue-green needles that curve upward, is another good choice for winter interest. Peren-nials, too, provide this foliage color: 'Jackman's Blue' rue, blue fes-cue, blue oat grass (*Helictotrichon sempervirens*) and Siebold hosta are a few popular choices. I like to grow deep wine-red, coral-pink, or pink flowers nearby.

Gray- and silver-leaved plants are plentiful and elegant. Weeping silver pear illuminates the spring and summer garden with its delicate, narrow willowlike leaves. Perennial artemisias, gray santolina, silver thyme, lamb's ears, lavender, and 'Beacon Silver' lamium add brightness through their foliage and cause nearby colors to become more radiant, especially pink, magenta, coral and orange.

Golden foliage is a bit trickier because it is brighter and bolder. A warm winter accent of golden hinoki cypress is as wel-come as a golden fall blaze of maidenhair tree (*Ginkgo biloba*) or a spring unfolding of yellow-green 'Sunburst' honey locust (*Gleditsia triacanthos* 'Sunburst'). Care needs to be taken in using yellow in summer's warmth; too much bright yellow can then be brassy. I keep golden foliage to a minimum in summer out of consideration for the many pink and magenta perennials that flower then.

Variegated foliage gives extra color when leaves are splashed or edged with white, cream, pink, or yellow, as in some forms of bugleweed (*Ajuga*), ivy, hosta, euonymus, acuba, andromeda (*Pieris*), hydrangea, and some of the ornamental grasses. One way to create intriguing combinations is to grow flowers that repeat the color of the variegation in the foliage nearby. Combine burgundy glow bugleweed (*Ajuga* 'Burgundy Glow') with pink-flowering masterwort (*Astrantia maxima*) to emphasize the bugleweed's pink variegation. Try the curled-leaf hosta (*Hosta crispula*) with its broad, dark green, white-margined leaves beside snowflake primrose (*Primula sieboldii* 'Snowflake') and white wood anemone (*Anemone nemerosa*) or snowdrop anemone (*Anemone sylvestris*) for a sophisticated green-and-white shade composition. The white flowers will echo the white margins of the hosta's leaves.

· MONOCHROMATIC, ANALOGOUS AND · COMPLEMENTARY COLOR SCHEMES

Monochromatic color schemes take one color and play with its various tints and shades. Sissinghurst's White Garden is the most famous of this kind of discipline and actually has flowers that are creamy-white, enhanced by gray, silver, blue-green, and green foliage. Using one color is restful, subtle, and encourages us to pay attention to form and texture. The shapes of flowers and plants become more noticeable when color is more subdued. It takes a refined sensibility and sophisticated understanding of texture and form to achieve this look. When done poorly, a monochromatic garden is simply monotonous.

Analogous color schemes combine neighboring colors on the wheel in a harmonious fashion. Melding blues, blue-violets, violets, and pink (a tint of red) creates a blend of related hues. Varying the values of these colors by using light tints and darker shades adds interest. Although it is safer to design with pastel colors, it is also likely to be a bit too bland. A good compromise for beginners is to let the pastels dominate and experiment with occasional accents of stronger, darker shades.

Complementary color schemes join opposites on the color wheel for a maximum of contrast. These opposite pairs are orange and blue, yellow and violet, and green and red. When these colors are of equal value, the results are electric. To reduce the vibrancy, you can use a tint of one with a medium shade of the other. For example, pale orange with cornflower blue, light yellow with eggplant purple, or pink with dark green. In the case of red flowers, their green foliage is often foil enough for a striking complementary picture.

What color schemes do I prefer? My garden is a series of ongoing experiments with color, texture, line, and form. Rather than one color scheme in my garden, I have a series of compositions that is like a collection of short stories. Some are more successful than others; the important part is the fun I have in the process of playing around to see what will happen.

· TEXTURE ·

When you look at fabric, you see all the colors and their patterns. An experienced fabric artist considers another quality: texture, the way the material feels. Is it smooth as satin, rough as wool, fine as silk, or soft as velvet? Plants are similar. They, too, have texture: a tactile quality that adds to their appeal and contributes another interesting facet to the garden.

The gallica rose 'Alain Blanchard' reminds me of old crushed velvet, with its deep burgundy petals and darker stains. 'Tuscany,' a gallica rose dating back to the sixteenth century, is commonly called 'Old Velvet Rose' for its rich maroon-red flowers. *Rhododendron yakusimanum* has leaves that look as if they've been dusted with confectionery sugar, and the undersides of the leaves are exactly like brown suede. Lamb's ears look and feel furry, and the richly colored bearded irises resemble purple, bronze, and maroon velvet. Some of the peonies and Icelandic poppies look silky; some roses and magnolias approach satin, oriental poppies are crepe-papery, and fall-flowering sedums (*Sedum spectabile*) are succulent and remind me of cauliflower. Foamflower (*Tiarella cordifolia*), meadow rue (*Thalictrum*) and baby's breath (*Gypsophila*) are like lace, while false spirea (*Astilbe*), meadowsweet (*Filipendula*) and white mugwort (*Artemisia lactiflora*) resemble feathery plumes. Sea holly (*Eryngium*) and globe thistle (*Echinops ritro*) are prickly coarse-textured plants that add dangerous excitement to a border.

So one element of texture is touch appeal. Another is how a plant reflects or absorbs light. The shiny leaves of Japanese aralia (*Fatsia japonica*) and southern magnolia (*Magnolia grandiflora*) reflect a lot of light and differ in texture from the flat green leaves of lilacs or apple trees.

Leaf size also contributes to texture. Large shiny English laurel leaves are bolder in texture than the smaller glossy leaves of camellias and sweet box (*Sarcococca*). Moss, the finest textured leaf is at one end of the spectrum, and bold-leaved *Gunnera* represents the coarser extreme.

Leaves can be folded, pleated, quilted or veined in ways that add to their texture. Folds in the leaves of David's viburnum or 'Dawn' viburnum, pleats in the bright green leaves of the rugosa roses, the quilted, blue-green leaves of Siebold hosta, all offer interesting textures. The gray leaves of *Geranium renardii* resemble elephant hide. Leaves of holly and Corsican hellebore are jagged edged, creating an eye-catching texture.

Thin-petaled flowers that allow light through have an especially wonderful translucency that makes their texture unique, something like stained glass. The flowers of annual painted tongue (*Salpiglossis*), single-flowered forms of opium poppy, Icelandic poppy, pink evening primrose (*Oenothera speciosa*) and 'Barnsley Pink' tree mallow (*Lavatera*) are a few examples of this texture.

Many trees have bark that has textural interest. The satiny mahogany-red trunk of birchbark cherry (*Prunus serrula*), the reddish-brown peeling bark of paperbark maple (*Acer griseum*) and the gnarled trunks of madrone (*Arbutus menziesii*) offer textural embellishment to the garden, especially welcome in the winter months.

Keep in mind that texture lasts far longer than color. Blossoms come and go, disappearing like confetti; but the leaves, stems, and bark of plants remain interesting for months, before and after flowering occurs. I think of bloom periods as Christmas, with all its dazzle and glitter—exciting enough, but here and gone, while the rest of the year (which is most of it) has to be enjoyed fully, too.

· LINE ·

"Line" signifies those features that point and direct the eye. Line can be angular or curved. Every plant, path, or garden structure can be thought of as a series of lines; and, in considering design, line is an important ingredient.

Where do you want the viewer to look? If you plan it that way, line will lead the eye to a vista, to a doorway, to a choice composition. You don't want a series of lines going up to the sky without a balance of horizontal lines to ground you and calm things down. Vertical lines create movement that can be restless alone, while horizontal lines soothe and anchor. Strong angular lines are crisp and definite, while curved lines are more gentle and flowing.

I lean toward curved lines and gradual transitions, with a resulting romantic garden with plants that billow and drape. I like to see the curve of a path, but I also like the plants to lap out over the pavement and weave together within the border.

You might prefer straight lines or crisper, tidier beds than I do, with clear separation between your plants. What I call "romantic," you might see as messy. This is a matter of personal taste.

To see how line exists in the garden, make a simple sketch of a garden space in winter. Notice how the tree trunks and branches are lines that go up, diagonally out, horizontally out, or perhaps arch downward. Observe the lines of paths and where they lead your eye. Pergolas, arbors, and arches, benches, fences, and gates, can also be reduced to two-dimensional lines. Do these lines relate well to each other? How is their balance? How is the transition between lines? Are you satisfied with how the lines flow in your garden? If not, what needs to be changed?

Wherever line takes you, make sure there is something of interest to follow. If a cherry tree weeps, pointing down, pay attention to what you place at ground level and consider a ground cover that enhances the arching lines to complete the picture. It will be disappointing to have it end in cedar chips, but lovely to

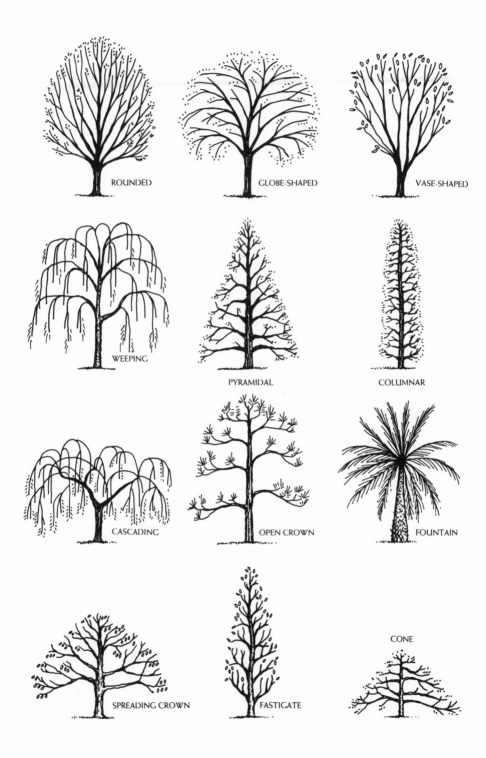

ROUNDED

GLOBE-SHAPED

VASE-SHAPED

WEEPING

PYRAMIDAL

COLUMNAR

CASCADING

OPEN CROWN

FOUNTAIN

SPREADING CROWN

FASTIGATE

CONE

have a carpet of cranesbill or bishop's hat or tulips as a final touch. If a path curves mysteriously, leading you to a bend through an arch, use the lines of that arch to frame a pleasing picture to delightfully surprise visitors as they enter the new space. If possible, let there be a sense of slow disclosure of the garden, an unfolding of separate spaces to enchant the viewer little by little.

· FORM ·

Form relates to the shapes of plants, structures, and garden ornaments. Form is similar to line, but is three-dimensional and tells us more about the volume of objects and how much space they occupy. If color in the garden is compared to painting, form can be likened to sculpture. When we think of plants and structures as forms, it will be easier to place them correctly, with adequate space between them. Form also helps us to stretch our minds to imagine the mature size of trees and shrubs, rather than the twiggy sticks that we plant in the ground. This takes some research; but without it, an overplanted jungle is inevitable. Visualizing form will help us create a better design instead of being limited to the individual personality of each plant. We will be able to see the forest *and* the trees.

Trees and shrubs generally have a few shapes that recur: rounded, pyramidal, vase-shaped, columnar, weeping, and prostrate, or flat-matted. Variety of shapes and contrast makes the garden interesting, but too much diversity creates commotion. Beginning gardeners often err on the side of too many trees and shrubs and too few massed areas of perennials, bulbs, and annuals, with the resulting effect of too many details and not enough simple strength. When in doubt, choose fewer trees and place them carefully with consideration for their ultimate size and shape. Select fewer kinds of shrubs, either grouping several of a kind together or repeating the same kind at intervals. Use perennials and annuals in drifts, rather than singly, considering the shape of the color mass that will result, rather than the beauty of each individual plant. Instead of flowers, think in terms of shapes filled with color, and you will be on the right track. Remember that the shapes of the plants will be there after the bloom color is spent.

When you get past the glamour of flower color, you will notice that flowers, too, have shapes. Rounded heads of peonies, poppies, globe thistle, lily-of-the-Nile (*Agapanthus*), summer phlox, and flowering onion (*Allium*) are quite different from the vertical spikes of bluebonnets (*Lupinus polyphyllus*), delphinium and pokers. Flat-headed plates of yarrow, autumn sedum, Japanese iris, and many of the daisy-shaped flowers create strong horizontal planes, while the ethereal flowers of baby's breath, meadow rue, crambe, and fennel are more amorphous and misty. Contrast between the columnar 'May Night' sage (*Salvia superba* 'May Night') and platelike moonshine yarrow creates drama in the garden. The nebulous haze of yellow fennel flowers makes a soft backdrop for the more definite, trumpet-shaped lilies. Elegant white chalices of calla lilies show up dramatically against the hazy spikes of yellow-white blue-eyed grass (*Sisyrinchium striatum*). Globe-shaped pink-red peonies stand out nicely against a solid carpet of blue-violet cranesbills (*Geranium ibericum*). A satisfying combination in my shade garden uses five *Hydrangea serrata* 'Preziosa' with strongly rounded reddish-purple flowers blooming behind masses of pink plume-shaped astilbe. The color scheme is harmoniously analogous, while the flower shapes offer enough contrast for some tension, blending comfort and excitement in equal proportions.

· SOME TOOLS FOR LEARNING ABOUT ·
COLOR COMBINATIONS

Early in my career I learned to carry a small notebook with me to list what was in bloom, by the month. I did this for several years and learned when plants bloomed and for how long. This is easier said than done, as the first task is to identify the beautiful tree with pink pendant flowers that you covet; then you can list it. As you keep track by the month, you begin to see which plants might be combined for a pleasing composition. You will also notice that in some years a plant might bloom earlier, or for a longer time. Temperature, rainfall, wind, vary enough to cause inconsistencies in flowering time. But there will still be an overall sequence of bloom and companions that usually bloom together. After a while you will know April brings flowering cherries and flowering crabapples and daffodils, while May means lilacs, eastern dogwoods and tulips. Writing things down also accelerates your learning process.

Landscape design instructor Dick Hollenbeck taught me to compose a calendar of color. This consolidated all the information from the little notebook into a master list by the month. To be more useful, the calendar should have each month's listings alphabetized and separated into trees, shrubs, perennials, bulbs, and ground covers. It's helpful to list the botanical name and common name, and to describe the important characteristics of each plant. This will be as good a reference guide for you as you make it.

A third tool that helped immensely when I began to design perennial borders is a finding list. This is for noting all the plants you want to include in a plan and seeing which bloom at the same time. Since the finding list has room for information about foliage

Perennials for a Blue and Yellow Garden

Botanical Name	Common Name	Color	Height	Bloom Time	Foliage	Remarks	Culture; Companions
Linum perenne	Blue Flax	blue	18"	spring; summer	delicate	short-lived but reseeds	nice filler plant, wafts around in breeze
Geranium wallichianum 'Buxton's Blue'	Buxton's Blue Cranesbill	blue with white eye	10"	spring; summer	small leaves	striking flowers	plant trails and drape, nice over a wall or near sidewalk
Aster x frikartii	Frikart's Aster	blue-lavender	3'	summer; fall	small, healthy leaves	long bloom period, cuts well	makes a small shrub; give it room to fill out to 3' across
Platycodon grandiflorum	Balloon-flower	blue	3'	summer	subtle	this emerges late in spring, be careful not to dig it out accidentally	slow to develop - be patient; great plant for long run
Lilium 'Golden Splendor'	Golden Splendor Lily	yellow	5'	summer	sturdy	fragrant big trumpet flowers	good drainage needed, bait for slugs when leaves emerge
Coreopsis 'Moonbeam'	Moonbeam Tickweed	light yellow	10"	summer; fall	delicate	use at front of border	
Sedum alboroseum 'Variegatum'	Variegated Sedum	pinkish	18"	fall	green, succulent, heavily marked with creamy yellow	use at front of border to show off striking leaves	easily propagated from tip cuttings

and height, it helps with decisions about textural compatibility and correct placement in the front, middle, or back of a bed or border.

One last way to get great color combinations is probably practiced by more gardeners than all the rest. It requires a shovel, a wheelbarrow, and guts. You notice several plants blooming in your garden at opposite ends of a bed or in different beds and suddenly realize that they would look terrific together. Decide where you would like to group them, make a written note to yourself, and mark the plants with ribbons to remind yourself later and make it easy to spot them. When the plants are done flowering, move them to change the picture to the one you want. When transplanting, prepare your new bed first; then move your plants from their old location. Do this in the coolest part of the day—preferably morning or evening—and water the plants well after the move.

Don't be afraid to experiment. Nature and art are your best teachers and will show you color combinations you might not have imagined. Some of the annual geraniums combine avant-garde colors. 'Kardinal,' with magenta petals, has orange markings at its center that electrify the magenta. The orbit series of geraniums has similarly scintillating representatives. In a massed planting of the annual painted tongue (*Salpiglossis*) or sweet william (*Dianthus barbatus*) you will see an amazing range of colors, tints, and shades that challenge all the rules of color use. Take heart and know that there is much to learn and experiment with. You will have some smashing successes, some mediocre combinations, a few occasional failures, and all the fun of playing around with color.

Four

. . . .

Planning

The planner will still make mistakes, many or fewer according

to his experience, but he will probably possess one tremendous

advantage: the capacity for visualizing how his plan will look

when it materializes. This capacity will have been won by his

having acquired the habit of observation, so that he can apply

the details of what he has seen and liked in the past to what he

means to create in his own garden. . . . Planning, moreover, goes

with a penchant for bold and generous grouping, as also

for repetition, in order to emphasize an effect.

—Christopher Lloyd

The Well-Tempered Garden

· · ·

· A CRITICAL SURVEY OF THE SITE ·

Most gardens that I help design have already been planted by a
previous homeowner. The first thing I do is take a stroll through

the garden with the current owner, clipboard and pencil in hand, asking questions and taking notes. "What do you like about this garden and what do you dislike? What are the strengths of this garden, and what are the problem areas? If you could have it look and feel exactly the way you wanted, what would it be like?"

I begin with general, open-ended questions, the same kind of questions I encourage you to ask yourself, to determine the theme, style and needed changes in your own garden. Then I go on to ask more specifically about likes and dislikes of existing bed shapes, existing trees, shrubs, and plant materials, and the way the design flows from one part of the garden to another. Before you refurnish, you have to clean house. Eliminate the structures, plants, and ornaments that don't work. Get rid of plants that are unhealthy, unattractive, or that you just plain don't like.

Some plants that are in the wrong place due to their size or sun/shade requirements can be listed to be removed and saved for other places where they would be more suitable. The ones you don't like can be removed or given away. It's your garden, and you deserve to have a place that you love and enjoy. You get no extra points for sentimentally saving the results of someone else's taste or poor planning. Learn from earlier mistakes, but don't continue to pay for them. If a plant has no beauty or function, think about taking it out. "What is that doing there?" is a question I ask a lot, as gently as I can. You should ask it of yourself as well.

Typically we begin with the front of the house, often looking from across the street to see the bigger picture. How does the size, shape, and style of the house relate to the landscape? Is the house connected to the ground by a canopy of trees and substory of shrubs? Can we see the front door, and is the path leading toward it inviting us to approach? Does the path flow in a pleasing line, and is it wide enough for two people to walk side by side? Are the plants near the front door attractive, interesting year-round, and are some of them fragrant? Can the residents see out the windows, or are light and view blocked by dense foundation plantings? Does the family have privacy from passersby, or can everyone outside stare into the house? How can we get light into the house, views out to the garden, and yet maintain some privacy? Which of the existing trees and shrubs should we keep, and which should be removed? Are the bed shapes graceful and ample enough, or do they need to be altered and, if so, how? Is there too much or too little grass?

From the front of the house, we move to the side and back yard and continue the discussion of garden features. Is the path leading us to the back adequate for foot traffic and convenient for wheelbarrows when needed? Is there enough privacy from neighbors, or do we need to plan fencing, screening shrubs, or hedges? What features in the back yard are satisfactory, and which need improvement? Is there enough space for seating, lounging, entertaining, playing, sports? Would the owner like a potting shed, greenhouse, cutting garden, dog run, wood-storage area, toolshed, or raised beds for vegetables? Is turf for active children desirable, or would the owner like to cut down on the amount of mowing by planning some colorful island beds?

It's important during this first walk through to identify areas of sun and shade. If you're not sure, spend some time to observe the light. This will help you figure out where to plan seating areas in spring's sunlight, and where to design lounging areas in the shade to enjoy during summer's heat. You need to know where the sun and shade are to make wise plant selections. It's amazing how often shade-loving rhododendrons are frying in the heat of a west exposure while sun-loving zinnias are silently mildewing and stretching their poor stems for light in the shade.

It's also important to notice the damp and dry places in the garden. Spongy ground and standing water on the surface indicate a high water table or poor drainage. These are places to plant water-loving plants, or to improve the drainage by creating raised beds above the ground, or by adding drainage pipes below the ground. Dry places are likely to be found under large trees, at the base of hedges and shrubs, and in sandy or rocky soil. These places can be landscaped with drought-tolerant plants, or the soil might be improved by adding peat moss, compost, or clay-based soil to better hold the moisture.

After touring the garden, it's just as important to walk through the house and notice which windows look out onto which areas of the garden. The views that you see daily from the kitchen, dining-room, and living-room windows will probably all need to be considered as frames for important garden pictures. Any window or sliding-glass door has potential for framing, and your plan should indicate these places with a small eye symbol (👁).

My primary job as a designer is to help gardeners dream up unique gardens that will give them ongoing pleasure without dampening their enthusiasm by constraints of time or money. However, once imagination is fired and flowing, there does come a time to ask the practical questions that will help us decide on more specific plants and structures. How much time do you have to garden? How much money is in the budget for plants, irrigation, paving, and construction of pergolas, arbors, or trelliswork? Is there money to hire help, or will you be doing it yourself? Will you do it all at once, or in stages? Do you want to plan the whole garden now, or plan one part, plant it, and then go on to the next part?

Asking these practical questions will help you make some decisions to get going and feel less overwhelmed. Most people have limits on their time and money, and setting priorities allows us to move forward within these limits. What is the most important place to design right now? That's where we begin. For most homeowners, I recommend planning in stages rather than tackling the entire garden. Perhaps a rough plan of the garden as a whole, a theme or style choice, or a rough sketch of areas and their uses is helpful. Then concentrating on one area at a time to plan thoroughly and plant is best. Unless you are highly experienced, you will learn much as you proceed, and your taste will develop and change—so avoid making all the decisions in the early stages of your garden education. I made my garden in stages over a period of six years, and I'm much happier with the results of my fourth year than my first. Making a garden can be a pleasure to savor rather than a rush job, and I urge you to give yourself ample time to make it a satisfying, thoughtful journey.

Building your garden one section at a time will also increase your confidence as you see the results of your efforts. It will leave something for you to look forward to and dream about. Considering your time and money allowances will permit you to make a garden that is affordable, instead of creating a burden for yourself.

· PLANNING ON PAPER ·

It's much easier to fiddle around on paper than in the garden. Pencils and erasers take much less energy to use than shovels and wheelbarrows. It's up to you how exacting your drawing needs to be. A sketch may be useful enough, or you may prefer an accurate plan, drawn to scale. Experienced gardeners are good at eyeballing distances, but even so it's helpful to measure the site carefully with a measuring tape or wheel, and then draw the house, site, and existing landscape features to get the overall picture. All you need is some gridded graph paper or drafting paper, and a ruler or a scale. Using a ruler and graph paper, you can let 1/4" or 1/2" on your ruler represent a foot in the garden to reduce your landscape to a manageable size. A scale is simply a sophisticated ruler that has built-in reductions, and allows you to draw any of a dozen or more reductions or enlargements of your original size.

Blueprint paper has the advantage of being available on rolls, but graph paper is just as serviceable, and 81/2" x 11" sheets can be taped together for a bigger drawing. Fade-out drafting paper is especially nice because the grid disappears when you copy the original, making the print easier to read. It is available in pad form and in rolls. A measuring tape of fiberglass or cloth is much easier to handle than the metal tapes that spring back and startle you silly. Investing in a measuring wheel will make your life simpler if you're going to do a lot of measuring on your own; but for occasional use, a tape is fine, and a helpful friend to hang onto the other end will come in handy. Without a helper, you can anchor the tape with a brick or by sticking a sharp stick through the end ring and into the ground. A compass, or a template of circular shapes, a two-foot flexible curve, or a piece of yarn will come in handy for drawing curves, circles and elipses.

Most drafted plans are drawn from an aerial point of view, as if you were a bird looking down on the garden. This gives you a two-dimensional schematic of the garden that you must translate in your mind's eye to a three-dimensional picture. For some people, a lot gets lost in the translation, and an elevation drawing, or one that shows a perspective that looks head-on at the garden, is more useful. This requires more drawing skill and knowing how to portray perspective, but can also be done roughly, just to get a fuller picture. Elevation drawings are especially useful in describing slopes, banks, terraces, raised beds, and stairs. Wherever there is a change in level, the garden will look different from above than below and elevation drawings will show you the varied views.

· MEASURING UP ·

To begin your drawing, whether drafted or sketched, take a blank sheet of paper out to the garden on a clipboard, with a pencil, eraser, and measuring tape. Take your time. Begin by drawing the outline of your house, carefully measuring the size and shapes of indentations, stairs, patios, landings, porches, and decks. Note where the windows and sliding glass doors are placed, how wide they are, and how high off the ground. This will show you where your views out are and prevent you from planting shrubs that are too tall in front of the windows. Draw in all doors, hose bibs, lighting structures, pumps, meters, and any other objects that will affect your design.

Then measure the perimeter of the property and note where there are fences, gates, and walls. Measure distances between the house and the perimeter at 90-degree angles, relating all corners of the house to the boundaries of your site. That will place your house correctly on the lot. Then sketch in the paths and beds that exist and measure their lengths and widths, and their distance to the house or perimeter, wherever you can at 90 degrees to either fixed point. Do the same with existing trees, and also measure the diameter of their canopies so that you will be able to draw them in aerially on the plan. To get an accurate position of a tree, measure its distance from a fixed corner of the house, and a fixed point in the fence line or some other structure. You can place it pretty accurately where those two distances intersect.

Make a note of which way north is on your map, like this: N

If there are significant slopes, banks, or dips, measure their dimensions and signify with a little arrow (↑) which way is up. If you can estimate whether it is a 30-, 45-, or 60-degree angle, make a note of your observations. If you notice that the ground is spongy or dry in a particular spot, or if a certain place needs screening, jot this down on the plan. Pencil in any observations about sun or shade, or the need to create sun or shade.

· DRAFTING TO SCALE ·

Transfer these measurements to graph or drafting paper, beginning by centering the property perimeter on the paper, next placing the house in accurate relationship to boundaries, and then tying in paths, driveways, patios, decks, stairs, trees and beds. Note placement of windows and doors by using an eye symbol, or by darkening the lines. Draw in the direction of north, and the scale you have chosen ($1/2''$ = 1', or $1/4''$ = 1'). Put 'remove' signs beside plants to be taken out.

You can use this original drawing by Xeroxing many copies of it and penciling in various plans, or by laying as many sheets of tracing paper on top of the original as you like until you are done experimenting. You can use paper to invent as many versions of your garden-to-be as you can dream up, and enjoy the process without fear of making mistakes. Take as much time as you need to innovate on paper.

· A FUNCTIONAL PLAN ·

Begin with a general plan to decide on where to place what. Let's say that you have decided that you need a sunny cutting garden, a sunny play area for the children, a potting shed, and a shaded sitting area for adults. The garbage cans need screening, the dog needs a run, and you want a compost bin that is out of sight but accessible by wheelbarrow. You spend a lot of time looking out of the kitchen and dining-room windows, and need shade to cool down the south-facing bedroom windows. Screening for privacy is important on the west property line.

With these desires in mind, you can begin to sketch in the possible ways to arrange these needed features in the garden, aiming for maximum usefulness, convenient access, and beauty. Perhaps you will design a potting shed that will also serve to screen compost bins to be built on the shed's far side. The children's play area might be defined by a circular paved path that will double as a tricycle track. The shady seating area might be placed under the same tree that will cool off the south-facing bedroom windows. Or you might prefer sliding glass doors that open the house to a brick patio for seating, with a plant-covered pergola overhead for shade.

You can play around on paper by using cutouts of the important feature areas and structures and moving them around on the paper, just as you'd move furniture around in a room. You can make simple shapes to represent a pergola, a dog run, a tree, island beds, a patio or deck, out of construction paper, and slide them around on your drawing until you're satisfied with the arrangement.

From time to time, as your plan is shaping up, check the views from windows and sliding glass doors. Is the scene you're creating in the garden enjoyable from these points of view? If you have a two-story home, imagine what you will see from the upper windows. Is there a tree canopy to look down upon, or a geometrically patterned herb garden? Think about how to create pleasing shapes and lines for viewing from the house, especially during the times of the year that you're indoors.

This is the time to note seasonal preferences on your plan. If you want a concentration of winter color near the entry and as a view from the kitchen window, jot this down on your drawing. If fragrance is a quality you want to include near the sitting areas or beside a bedroom window, make a note on the plan.

Borrowed landscape is a bonus in many gardens. These are views of neighboring sites that can look as if they are part of your garden picture, if you plan properly. If you're lucky enough to have a mountain or river in sight, note where they are in your plan so that you can create a vista in their direction. My neighbor's garden has a huge weeping willow that I use as backdrop for mixed borders of shrub roses and perennials. By purposely keeping the fence line between our properties low (4') and fairly invisible (post and wire mesh) I have created the illusion that my garden is deeper and is continuous with my neighbor's. This works in all seasons but winter, when the leaves drop and I see fence posts, tree trunks, and his house. Had he only planted a deodar cedar, we both would have year-round privacy; but I am content with the willow's grace.

· PATHS ·

When you arrive at a pleasing arrangement of areas and structures, begin to draw in paths. Getting around in your garden should strike a balance between convenience and beauty. A garden is a place for relaxation and inspiration—not a freeway—so paths can meander and wind, with bends to offer surprises and stopping points to stand or sit and admire the view, plants, and fragrances. Paths serve as decorative elements in the garden, especially if they are built of attractive stone, slate, or brick. Japanese gardens, in which pathways are elevated to an art form, are excellent showcases for studying texture, line, and layout of paths.

Let the path lines be graceful and proportionate to neighboring features. Avoid busy, fussy lines; favor broad sweeps and generous stretches that take both foot and eye in a purposeful direction, toward a door, bench, vista, border, enclosure, or focal point.

· THE SPECIFIC PLAN ·

With your general layout on paper, you are now ready to select your plants. Notes will tell you where you need shade, canopy, and screening. For these places, consider trees or structures tall enough to fill those functions. Where privacy is needed, consider shrubs for screening, or a hedge. Begin to form the canopy and walls of your garden with trees, shrubs or fences, and walls. When the bigger trees and shrubs are decided upon, their character, bloom period, and texture will help you choose perennials, bulbs and ground covers to complement them.

Do your homework before selecting a tree. The tree will be there for decades, and so will you, looking at it; so spending a few hours of your time on research is a good investment. Don't take the attitude that you will be living in your home for only five years, and then moving. Life hands us many surprises, and often we are still there twenty years later and so is the tree we chose so carelessly, much to our chagrin.

Look through as many tree books as you can to see photographs and find out what appeals to you visually. Get to know what each tree you like offers, both aesthetically and functionally. What is its ultimate height, spread, and shape? When does it bloom and for how long? Does it set ornamental fruit or cones? What about fall color, winter bark, and branching patterns? When does it leaf out, and when does it drop its leaves? Is the shade it casts dense or filtered? Is the root system deep or shallow? Does it tend to sucker, break easily in wind or ice storms, drop messy fruit or stickery pods? Is it usually susceptible to aphids, virus, or fungus? How long is it likely to live? What are its pruning requirements? Aim for a healthy tree that grows slowly but steadily to the size you are seeking, with at least two seasons a year of interest.

Visit mature trees in gardens and parks to get a sense of their character. If you can wait, look at the trees you're considering at different seasons. Don't let the season during which you are designing influence you unduly. Everyone falls in love with flowering cherries in the spring. Consider what a tree will offer you throughout the year.

Ask yourself whether you want an evergreen or a deciduous tree, and what the advantage of each would be in the place you're planting. How do the shapes and interesting features of each compare? Do you want the solid bulk of an evergreen, or the changing form of a deciduous tree?

An analytical person can start the search with list of traits, knowing that the tree desired is spring blooming, with a rounded head, interesting bark, and with small enough leaves to disintegrate easily, making raking minimal. Then a quick search through books will offer several trees that meet these requirements, and one will be found to be the best of the lot.

Choosing your shrubs comes next. Evergreen shrubs are the answer where you want year-round leaves, or complete screening for privacy. Deciduous shrubs belong where you want a burst of seasonal color and where winter dormancy is acceptable. Typically, entry areas call for a greater proportion of evergreens, while back yards are likely to call for more deciduous shrubs.

For a more effective result, plan groups of three, five, or seven shrubs. Instead of lining them up like soldiers, triangulate them: plant two forward, with one behind and between the forward two, in a triangular pattern. This gives a thick, full look, instead of a narrow line.

Function will help you decide on the kind of shrub and how many of a kind. A privacy screen will call for plants of a specific height, tall enough to block out the offending structure. The sun or shade requirements of the site will also influence your choices. For example, a south-facing property line needs screening from a neighbor's yard. You will be spending time in that part of the garden in summer and fall. Deciduous shrubs six to eight feet tall with sun-loving flowers that bloom summer and fall will fit the bill. All of these requirements can be met by rugosa, Bourbon or English roses.

The shadier, northeast perimeter of your garden needs an eight-foot-tall screen to hide an unsightly wood-storage area. You want complete privacy during all four seasons. Evergreen shrubs that are shade loving are in order here. Tall rhododendrons or camellias will work well and give you the added bonus of spring flowers.

If trees are the ceiling and shrubs are the walls, then ground covers, perennials, annuals, and bulbs are the carpet of your outdoor room. For some of us, the ground is rich as an oriental carpet and takes a lot of planning because we are color and texture conscious, and love details. Others prefer a simple carpet that is secondary to the main features. This is a style choice. The ground can be designed with elaborate perennial borders or intricate herbal knot gardens. Masses of bulbs or ground covers in simpler design patterns, pools and drifts of color forward of the shrubs or around the trees can be equally beautiful.

· PLANNING IN THE GARDEN ·

I prefer to plan right in the garden because there are so many details that get lost on paper: a distant view, the angle of light, the wind, the way the atmosphere feels in a certain part of the garden. For the overall layout of beds, borders, and paths, I wander around at first, looking from all angles. After a while I might zero in on a certain part of the garden and take a chair there and sit and stare aimlessly. Nothing else is important at this time; my full relaxed attention concentrates on noticing what is in front of me. I begin to see that a certain tree I have always looked at—but not really seen—is quite beautiful and would be even more graceful if I pruned out some awkward branches. It could serve as a focal point of a sizable bed, set off to one side and underplanted with shade-loving low shrubs and perennials. Since this tree flowers in spring, I'd like to make the bed a spring picture, so I'll choose shrubs and perennials that also flower then, and add some spring-flowering bulbs as well. To carry interest into the next season, I'll overplant the bulbs with a summer-flowering ground cover.

Or it might be that the tree I stare at is misshapen, and I remember how small and sour its fruits were. I realize that I don't like it one bit and want to take it out. This leaves me a clear, sunny area to work with, and I've always wanted to grow David Austin's English roses. I begin to imagine a mixed border of pink-and-white English roses, with fragrant lavender and blue-violet Frikart's asters, all summer flowering.

Sometimes the starting point will be a need for screening a neighboring house or garage from view. This will determine placement of a tree, hedge, or structure. In screening, perspective is important. The closer a screen is to your eye, the larger it will appear; the farther away, the smaller. Notice how much more your hand screens out when it is close to your face, and how that changes when you move it away from you. This is why courtyard walls close to the house will do a better job screening the road than the same-size walls placed closer to the road.

To determine how high a screen is needed, you must see it from the place you will be looking from. Are you looking out the window, from the patio, or from halfway down the garden? Stand there and look. To simulate a screen, plant a tall stake, or ask someone to stand where you want the screening tree or fence. Squint and see whether that height will be sufficient. If not, add to it. Ask the person to lift the stake above his head. You can get about twelve feet of height that way. Is that tall enough? I imagine several six-foot-tall people stacked up if I need to think really tall, to get a rough idea of heights. You can also get a quick rough estimate of height by using a nearby tree or fence as a mental yardstick.

Since it is difficult to move a tree once it is planted, and it will be there for a long time, consider its ultimate height, spread, and root system carefully before committing yourself. Its canopy will create shade, its roots will take up space both downward and outward, so the ground beneath will be dry and shady, affecting nearby plants. To be certain about correct placement, I like to plant a stake where I think a tree will go and leave it there for a while. That way I have a chance to view it from all sides and imagine how it will look from different parts of the garden. It's a lot easier to move the stake around or take it out if I change my mind.

Sometimes there will be a fine view that you want to frame by building an arch or a gate, an arbor or a pergola. To check a view, make a frame by putting your thumbs and index fingers together. Close one eye and look. Do you like the picture?

There are many ways to learn to see. I learned a lot about framing by photographing gardens. Looking through the lens of a camera teaches you to compose the picture by including the beautiful composition that's planted in one corner of the bed and leaving out the mess that's nearby. Borders will look different seen from ground level, straight on or from above, so photographers spend time on their knees, bellies, up on ladders, or moving their cameras around on tripods. It's the same for you in the garden: things will look different if you are sitting on the ground, on a chair, walking around, or looking from an upstairs window. Think this through when planning.

When you are planning the shape of beds, borders, and paths, use hoses to try out curves. Give them a chance to warm up in the sun for maximum flexibility, then start moving them around and playing with shapes. For long stretches, you may need to connect two or more hoses. Leave them out for a day or two while you think things over. How does the shape look from different places as you wander around the garden? Adjust the lines all you like before making a final decision.

For straight lines, use stakes and string. Some gardeners use spray paint to try out lines, but of course these are harder to erase. Sand might be a better bet.

There's no harm in waiting if you're not sure about the light, the drainage, or your own desires. Gardens of lasting beauty often require a year or more of looking and planning before taking action. Most good things take time.

While you are in the planning stages, you can take action of another sort out in the garden. Make a holding bed filled with rich, crumbly soil, somewhere in the back of the garden. As you begin to decide on the plants you *must* have in the garden, while you are deciding on their exact placement, buy them and plant them in the holding bed. That way, by the time you are ready for planting, you will have bigger, healthier specimens. The loose soil in the holding bed makes it easy to move the plants when you are ready. This is a way to get started and indulge your love of plants without planting them in their permanent positions prematurely.

Without a holding bed, you can accomplish similar goals by potting newly arrived plants in ample containers (two-, three-, or five-gallon pots) so that they can spread their roots freely and grow. If you anticipate a severe winter, you may want to protect them from freezing by plunging them into a bed of sawdust, or holding them in a cold frame.

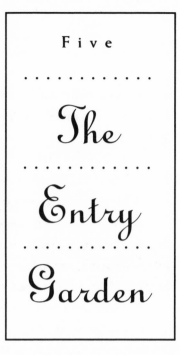

Five

. . . .

The

. . . .

Entry

. . . .

Garden

It will require the finest food and the most comfortable

chair to make up for being obliged to walk through mud,

or having your hat knocked off by overhanging trees and

your stockings ripped on the pyracantha.

—Thomas Church

Gardens are for People

. . .

The entry welcomes guests to your home. So many of us go from the car, through the garage to the interior of our homes that it's easy to forget how the entry feels to a visitor. Take a walk from the road to your front door. Can you find your way easily? Is the path wide enough for two? Is the surface steady and stable? Are your clothes safe from menacing thorns and wet shrubbery over-hanging the path? Having visited many homes for consultations, I have slipped on wet brick, skated on wet wooden decks, stag-gered on wobbly stepping-stones, slid on gravel paths, and tripped on awkward steps. Wet brick and wood can be treacher-ous, as slippery as ice. Gravel and stepping-stones are likely to shift underfoot, especially on inclines. For important paths lead-ing to your entry, choose a paving material that is firm and offers traction. Exposed aggregate is a favorite for its muted color that cuts down on bright sun's glare, and its rough texture that pro-vides adequate friction for traction when it's wet. Crushed rock, firmly tamped down, makes a good secondary path in the outly-ing areas, but is too inviting to weed seeds that sprout in it to make a good main path. Gray or black stones, chosen carefully for flatness, can be handsome. Whether you choose poured concrete, pavers, or stone, have the work done by a reputable professional whose finished work you have seen. There is a world of difference between an ample, well-made path and a flimsy attempt. The en-try is a place to do things right.

Entries are strongly affected by cars and parking needs. In some cases, circular driveways and three- or four-car garages are strong elements of the existing architecture, and should be con-sidered when planning the garden. Do the best you can to make these features part of the garden. A garage can be dressed up with vines to soften its structure. Brick lends itself to Virginia creeper (*Partheonocissus quinquefolia*) or Boston ivy (*Parthenocissus tricuspidata*). With a little imagination, sides and backs of wooden garages can be transformed into garden features. A door and windows can be treated to suggest a cottage by adding window boxes and containers filled with colorful annuals and bulbs. A circular driveway can feature an island bed at its center, planted with one tree off center and low-growing shrubs or ground covers. This will give a sense of garden welcome in the midst of functional paving. Fragrant witch hazel (*Hamamelis mollis*), 'Dawn' viburnum (*Viburnum bodnantense* 'Dawn'), or sweet box (*Sarcococca*) can waft a fragrant greeting well before you see them.

Paths to the front door can take a variety of shapes. One common pattern is a straight path at right angles to the driveway, parallel to the front of the house. This is a practical solution for people parking in the driveway; they can leave the car and walk directly to the front door. In terms of garden space, this path design divides the entry garden into a narrow rectangular bed between the path and the house, and a larger rectangular bed between the path and the road. It also means that the pedestrian on this path sees the narrow bed closer to the house, and the larger bed toward the road, but is not being taken through the garden so much as being shot to the front door.

For people who are more garden centered, additional paths taking the visitor through the entry garden are more inviting. A straight path from curb to front door at right angles to the curb that divides the entry space into two equal rectangles lends a formal geometric look. For symmetry, the left and right sides of this space would mirror each other, if not in exactly the same plants, perhaps in bed shapes or plant shapes and sizes. To increase the sense of welcome, frame a straight path on both sides with low-growing edging plants, such as lavender, or dwarf boxwoods. A low fence with a gate opening onto the path, or an arbor with flowering climbers overhead could further define the feeling of moving into a garden room.

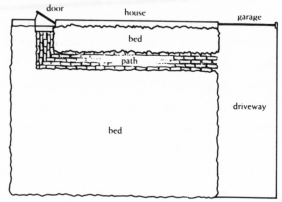

Typical driveway with path to front door
dividing space into narrow and wide rectangles

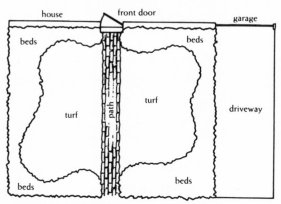

Path divides entry into two rectangles

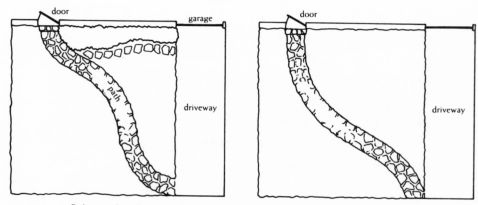

Path curves from driveway to front door, dividing space into two triangles, and taking visitor
through the garden

A curved path from one corner of the curb to the front door, dividing the entry space into two roughly triangular shapes is another option. This takes the visitor more slowly through the garden and adds the grace of a curved line to the garden design. Framing the path with edging plants will emphasize the curve. As curves are more informal than straight lines, a variety of edging plants, instead of just one kind, could be selected for a more casual look. For a cottage-garden style, pave a path wider than needed and plant edging perennials that spill over onto the pavement, bringing color and fragrance to the visitor's feet. Brushing against lavender and thyme, and enjoying the clove scent of cottage pinks will be your guest's first welcoming impressions of your garden.

· TREES FOR THE ENTRY ·

It is worth everything to be able to see

your house through the arch of a tree.

—Thomas Church

Gardens are for People

There is something about a tree's canopy and graceful branches that says permanence, protection, shelter, and makes a home feel like a castle. A house standing by itself looks isolated, a man-made box dropped onto the surface of the earth. Framed by a tree, a house is linked to the landscape and related to nature. Whether in a circular drive, on the front lawn, or in a bed near the entry, a tree embellishes and softens the strict lines of architecture with the pattern of its leaves. The visitor is welcomed; the resident inside looks out to enjoy a tree's presence.

Small-leaved deciduous trees with open branching afford privacy from inside the house without robbing you of too much light, especially in winter, when light is essential. Depending on its canopy size and the depth and width of its root system, a tree should be placed far enough from the house to avoid damaging its foundation and pathways. Aesthetically, a tree is placed to advantage forward of—and in line with—the corners of the house to soften its vertical lines, or where its shape and size are needed to balance an equivalent mass. A view out an important window might also determine its placement. A big-enough home on a sizable lot might call for several trees. Repeating the same tree can be unifying to the design. A two-story brick home with three zelkova trees planted in the entry garden makes a powerful partnership of architecture and nature. For more information on specific trees and their functions, see Chapter 7.

· SHRUBS ·

Evergreen shrubs lend year-round greenery to the entry. Select plants low enough to let the windows serve their purpose, with an ultimate spread that fits your bed. For fragrance, daphnes are irresistible, especially 'Carol Mackie' daphne with variegated leaves and lavender-pink flowers. The bronze-leaved evergreen huckleberries (*Vaccinium ovatum*) will give you the added bonus of edible fruit. Shiny deep-green leaves of four-foot-tall Japanese convex-leaf holly (*Ilex crenata 'Convexa'*) makes a handsome entry statement. 'Helleri,' its dwarf cousin, makes a shapely green mound the size of a small azalea, but hardier. For variegated foliage, the evergreen variegated boxwood (*Buxus sempervirens 'Aureovariegata'*) and colorful 'Emerald Gaiety,' euonymus with its pink, green, and burgundy leaves, are appealing. Where a little more height is needed, five-foot-tall heavenly bamboo (*Nandina domestica*) offers upright form, lacy white flowers in the spring and red berries in the fall. David's viburnum (*Viburnum davidii*) with its handsome lined leaves, white Queen Anne's lace-type flowers, blue berries, and reddish stems, is useful where its wide spread (five feet and more) is desirable. Normally taller and wider (six by six), pliable Mexican orange (*Choisya ternata*) is pruned easily to smaller dimensions. Its bright-green, glossy leaves and fragrant white flowers make it an easy companion to combine with other shrubs and perennials.

If your entry is shady, consider the dwarf rhododendrons, dwarf forms of mountain laurel (*Kalmia latifolia* hybrids) or dwarf sweet box (*Sarcococca hookeriana humilis*). Sweet box has tapered, glossy, dark-green leaves and fragrant, small white flowers that bloom in winter, followed by shiny dark blue-black berries.

Where you need more height, camellias, larger rhododendrons, and Japanese aralia (*Fatsia japonica*) with its large, shiny, tropical leaves reminiscent of fig trees, make bold textural accents in an entry garden. Clusters of white flowers rise at the tops of the aralia in fall and change into inky black berries that are useful as dye. But keep *Fatsia* away from pavement unless you want it dyed blue-black.

You might like the embellishment of a needle evergreen or two in your entry. They will contribute year-round foliage color and definite shapes to the garden. The dwarf balsam fir (*Abies balsamea* 'Nana') has deep-green glossy needles and makes a handsome rectangular shape, about two feet tall and twice as wide. The bird's-nest spruce (*Picea abies* 'Nidiformis') is a three-foot-tall flat-topped shrub, much wider than tall, spreading to five or six feet across. The new foliage is bright green, and although a young plant may remind you of a bird's nest, remember to allow ample room because the mature plant will grow to the size of a coffee table. Its beauty lies in the dense, horizontally layered branches that add pattern to the garden, and its unique shape is best enjoyed as a specimen rather than hemmed in by other plants. Dwarf forms of Hinoki cypress are upright and pyramidal, with irregular branching patterns that are intriguing. *Chamaecyparis obtusa* 'Nana Gracilis' is the most popular dwarf Hinoki cypress, growing fairly soon to its three foot tall by two foot wide size.

For a spectacular specimen entry plant, the weeping blue Atlas cedar (*Cedrus atlantica* 'Glauca Pendula') can stand alone. Trained to a sturdy trellis, it resembles year-round sculpture, with striking blue clusters of needles, gracefully pendant. One plant, trained to a tall arbor, can frame an entry or arch over a driveway, charming the visitor.

· PERENNIALS ·

Perennials and bulbs can add color and texture to your entry. Some are as architectural as garden ornaments; a few are evergreen and of year-round interest. The low-growing hellebores are evergreen and winter blooming, with striking foliage to boot. Lenten rose (*Helleborus orientalis*) is the most popular, with pink, cream, or maroon flowers that open in February and flower into April. Bold, glossy, medium-green handlike leaves add strong pattern to an entry garden. The Corsican hellebore (*Helleborus lividus corsicus*) has dark green leaves with finely jagged edges and pale yellow-green winter flowers. Tropical-looking bear's-foot hellebore (*Helleborus foetidus*) has handsome dark green pinwheel-shaped leaves. Its pale green blossoms look as if someone had run a very fine paintbrush dipped with red ink on the rim of the flower. Hellebores form seed pods in late spring, and by summer shiny black seeds begin to explode out of the papery pods, landing under the mother plant. To encourage seed germination, mulch around the plants with a top dressing of compost, and next winter, as you cut away last year's old leaves, you will see a host of seedlings.

Bergenia, with its bold cabbagelike evergreen leaves and winter flowers in shades of pink, magenta and white, is a valuable perennial for the entry. Underplanted with evergreen bugleweed (*Ajuga reptans*) with its smaller, flat leaves, and clumps of early snowdrops (*Galanthus*), or early-flowering daffodils (*Narcissus* 'February Gold' or 'Tete-a-Tete'), an entryway would give a warm winter welcome. There are many forms of bugleweed to enhance an entry garden. 'Burgundy Glow' has leaves colored with shades of white, pink, rose, and green. 'Silver Beauty' has gray-green leaves with white edges; 'Atropurpurea' has dark bronzy-purple leaves. These bugleweeds flower with spikes of bluish-purple flowers in spring, and the plants grow rapidly in sun or shade, dry or wet. Their aggressive nature is their only drawback, and although they are easy enough to pull out of beds where they have migrated, they are best kept away from lawns.

Bishop's hat (*Epimedium*) is a delightful evergreen ground cover with heart-shaped leaves and small spring-blooming flowers in shades of yellow, pink, and white. Its tolerance for deep shade and dry soil is noteworthy, as is its open growth habit on long, wiry stems, that allows small leaf litter to fall through and disappear downward. This is a ground cover for gardeners who would rather not rake.

A few additional low-growing spring bloomers with evergreen leaves are evergreen candytuft (*Iberis sempervirens*), foamy bells (*Heucherella tiarelloides*), coral bells (*Heuchera sanguinea*), 'Palace Purple' coral bells (*Heuchera micrantha* 'Palace Purple'), Mrs. Robb's spurge (*Euphorbia robbiae*), and wall rock cress (*Arabis albida*). All of these are sun and shade tolerant, with the exception of 'Palace Purple' coral bells and Mrs. Robb's spurge, which prefer shade. 'Palace Purple,' with reddish-brown leaves shaped like ivy, makes a bold color accent at the edge of a shady bed. Mrs. Robb's spurge not only likes shade but thrives in *dry* shade, traveling quietly underground in the poorest soil, even at the base of densely rooted trees. Its dark blackish-green leaves form rosettes, and unusual, greenish-yellow flower bracts rise up in spring, like visitors from another planet. It is well enhanced by the bear's-foot hellebore.

The more conventional coral bells have lovely lobed leaves, sometimes marbled with silver, and pink, red, or white flower spikes. The closely related foamy bells also have lobed leaves and salmon-pink flowers. A variety named 'Bridget Bloom' has clear pink flowers that bloom for months. Evergreen candytuft with dark green leaves and wall rock cress, with gray-green leaves, both have white flowers and tend to spread and sprawl. Ideally, these are plants to drape over the edge of a wall, rock garden, or ample, paved path.

· ENCLOSING THE ENTRY ·

Often the sunniest, most inviting part of the garden sits between the house and the road, and although it would make the best outdoor living space or growing area, lack of privacy stops you from using it well. There it sits, like the old-fashioned parlor, rarely used, but for show when company comes. With space becoming increasingly precious, consider the option of enclosing the entry to make it private and more useful.

A covered gate, stone path, and small pool
announce the Japanese style of this enclosed
entry garden designed by Stephen T. Carruthers.

A modest, newly built one-story home has its front garden enclosed by a simple, solid, five-foot-tall wooden fence. The entry is marked by a covered gate in the Japanese style. In Japan this kind of gate would have a tile roof, and by placing 1" × 2" battens, or narrow strips of wood, over 1' × 6' boards, designer Stephen Carruthers achieved a pattern that looks like tile. Flat gray stones form a landing forward of the gate and continue to pave the path leading to the front door. Japanese bloodgrass, dwarf heavenly bamboo, and needle evergreens are planted on the street side to welcome the visitor and dress up the plain fence. A ceramic wall piece reminiscent of a sand dollar, and a weathered bell anchored to the gate add textural detail. Lacy fronds of black bamboo peek over the fence from inside the courtyard, softening the vertical house corner like a willowy tree.

Walk through the gate to enjoy patterns of smooth stone on the ground with planting pockets of Corsican mint, a small pool backed by the black bamboo, and grassy-leaved Siberian iris repeating the bamboo's vertical rhythm at the pool's forward edge. Ceramic fish perched on iron rods swim silently through the grassy foliage, reminding us of koi (ornamental goldfish). Tasteful clumps of red and golden grasses, and a small glossy-green Japanese holly rise up above a carpet of gray woolly thyme. Flowering pomegranate with orange flowers is espaliered against the house, and a small simple wooden bench invites you to sit and contemplate the scene. The front door, with its older-looking wooden screen door, welcomes you, and the handle, handmade from a rhododendron branch, is another detail to remind you what a labor of love the garden is. Heavenly bamboo at one side of the porch, and a carefully chosen stone on the other side echo the Japanese touches found earlier. By enclosing the entry, the owner has transformed formerly public space into a private oasis of tranquillity.

Entirely different in style, a stately two-story colonial home has an entry garden surrounded by a six-foot-tall, formally clipped holly hedge. An inviting white picket gate is the only break in the solid green wall: open the gate and you may walk straight ahead to the front door; but unless you are blind, you won't. Inside the entry garden, lush perennial borders flower against the walls of hedges, as opulent as the hedges are strict. What might have been a conventional lawn has been transformed into a cottage garden, with fragrant, colorful plants everywhere. A curved path branches off the main entry path and tempts you to wander toward the back garden. You catch glimpses of rose beds, perennial borders, and an arbor by peeking over the next gate, and soon open it to explore further. The garden unfolds slowly, in an irresistible progression of scenes. You are led down the garden path, lured further by glimpses and scents of what is next to be revealed. A sheltering gazebo beckons.

If you decide to hedge in your entry garden, keep in mind that evergreen plants with relatively small, subtle leaves are best. Avoid rampageous growers such as English laurel or photinia; they will create maintenance headaches. Choose slower-growing plants that top out at the desired height and exercise patience, or you will get more exercise pruning than you will enjoy. Fine-textured conifers such as arborvitae (*Thuja occidentalis*), yew (*Taxus baccata, Taxus media*), incense cedar (*Calocedrus decurrens*), and Canadian hemlock (*Tsuga canadensis*) provide soothing green backdrop without distracting flowers.

Large broadleaf evergreen shrubs can act as screens, effectively walling in an entry garden in a less formal way. They will

take up more space and require less pruning than hedges. Tall rhododendrons and camellias screen well in shade. In sun, evergreen
Euonymus, Laurustinus (*Viburnum tinus*), Japanese holly (*Ilex crenata*),
and English holly (*Ilex aquifolium*) are serviceable. Andromeda
(*Pieris japonica*) is lovely in partial shade. Avoid shrubs with big,
glossy leaves if you plan to grow beds or border in front of them,
as their shinier leaves will detract from the beauty of companion
flowers. Remember that hedges and screens are green backdrop
walls, and be sure that they keep their secondary place.

Constructed walls, fences, and baffles are initially more ex-
pensive solutions to privacy, but will save you time and labor in the
long run. Brick and stone are choice materials that give a feeling of
immediate age to a garden; their colors and textures complement
the garden's greenery. Climbing roses, honeysuckle, and clematis
can be trained up against these walls if desired. Planting pockets
may be left in stone walls for cascading perennials and annuals:
cottage pinks, sedums, thymes, portulaca, campanula, sunroses,
cranesbills, and many more. Walls are ideal backdrops for perennial borders. Be sure to leave room between the wall and the border
so that you can walk there to prune, weed, and fertilize. Design
the border so that it is in scale with the wall; the taller the wall, the
deeper the border, and the taller the back border plants should be.

If you are sensitive to subtleties in color, pay attention to the
details. Notice that some brick is slightly orange, some more
pink, and be aware of which you prefer. Stone varies in color and
texture: it can be pale yellow, gray, nearly black or even greenish.
Select the stone that best enhances your home and garden.

Walls of concrete reflect a lot of light and usually benefit
from plant patterns, whether vines, such as Virginia creeper, wall
shrubs, or espaliered plants. A trellis can be bolted to a wall for

training roses or other climbers. Allow spacers between the wall and trellis to assure good air circulation.

Wooden fences can be decorative as well as functional, with posts and rails creating rhythmic patterns. Solid fences offer full privacy, but darken and cast shade. Partially open fences compromise the screening, but admit air and light. Split-rail and picket fencing set their own moods; but although they suggest a boundary, neither offers much privacy.

Baffles—a series of upright panels—offer some privacy without full enclosure. They remind me of room partitions that separate without closing off. Baffles repeat, so there is rhythm in their progression.

Other combinations can also screen the entry. A low brick wall with a street-side avenue of trees joins the garden wall and canopy to ensure privacy from the street and a pleasing view of leafy branches from the house. A mixed border of trees and shrubs—some evergreen and some deciduous—can give some privacy and a lot of seasonal color.

If you choose to enclose your entry with a fence, hedge, or wall, think about leaving at least a bed's depth on the street side to plant as a welcoming public border. Before deciding how to design your entry, ask yourself how private you want it to be and how much of it you are willing to share with the outside world.

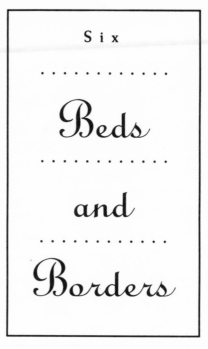

Six

Beds

and

Borders

Gardening is largely a question of mixing one sort of plant
with another sort of plant, and of seeing how they marry
happily together; and if you see that they don't marry happily,
then you must hoick one of them out and be quite ruthless about
it. That is the only way to garden. The true gardener must be
brutal, and imaginative for the future.

—Vita Sackville

West's Garden Book

The best gardening, as I see it, achieves a tapestry

of plants. All the units touch or intermingle

and no canvas shows through.

—Christopher Lloyd

· · ·

Just as paintings are arranged on a variety of canvas sizes and shapes, garden pictures are composed within the frame of beds and borders. Beds and borders come in various styles. Island beds are freestanding areas, surrounded by either lawn, paved surfaces, or gravel. Because you can walk around island beds and view them from all sides, designing them requires all the attention to detail that goes into a freestanding flower arrangement. Borders are usually made against the backdrop of a hedge, wall, fence, or house, and are viewed mostly from one side. Less perfection is required, especially from the places farther away from the front.

The shapes of your beds and borders will contribute to the overall garden design as much as the plants within them. Geometric shapes may be planned: rectangular, square, triangular, circular, and eliptical are most common. If the garden allows, more elaborate shapes can be chosen, for example L-shaped, U-shaped and crescent-shaped beds. One traditional pattern with three concentric circles forms an inner circular bed, a path around it, and an outer circular bed interrupted by an entry and an exit. Another design sets two concentric circles inside a rectangle. The middle circle and outer rectangle are interrupted to create entry and exit paths. Four L-shaped beds can be arranged to form a

Garden Patterns

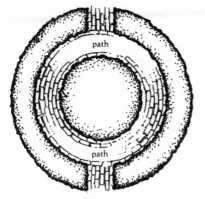

path

path

3 concentric circles

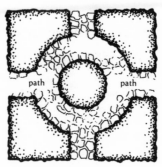

path   path

2 concentric circles within a rectangle

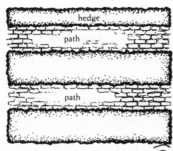

path

2 triangular beds

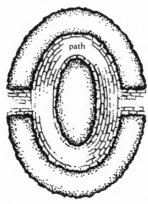

path

2 horseshoes with central island

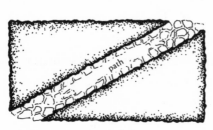

hedge

path

path

2 rectangular beds with hedge

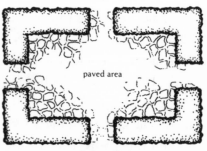

paved area

4 L-shaped beds

Viewed from here - the eye symbol is indicating that the viewer looks at these two beds with a hedge behind them from this point of view, thus seeing the picture as a big bed backed by a hedge, and not seeing the paths in between.

symmetrical pattern, or two horseshoes can mirror each other with a central island between them. Two rectangular beds with a path between them, a path and a hedge behind them can give the illusion of a very deep border, yet have ample access to weed, groom, and prune.

Beds and borders can be filled with a mixture of trees, shrubs, perennials, bulbs, and annuals, or can be limited to one or two of these plant groups. Similarly, one bed can have four seasons of interest within it, with a color scheme for each season, or can focus entirely on one season of bloom. The complexity of design is up to you, your level of expertise, and the amount of work you wish to take on. Knowing the specific purposes of your beds and borders will help you determine the kinds of plants needed as well as their bloom seasons, heights, shapes, and color schemes. A bed to screen out the summer compost pile will be tall, with summer-flowering shrubs and perennials dominating, while an entry bed might have a larger proportion of winter-flowering, low-growing, evergreen perennials and dwarf shrubs.

Traditional English borders were made to show off the choice plants beloved by expert gardeners in a period when money, time, and skilled help were plentiful. Elaborate artistic endeavors, these borders were typically grand in scale, backed by clipped hedges of yew or beech and filled with perennials, shrubs, vines, and bulbs. Behind the scenes in such gardens were cold frames and greenhouses to grow plants from seeds and cuttings, ensuring a good supply of unusual annuals and half-hardy perennials. Any seasonal gaps in color could be filled easily by a quick trip to the greenhouse to grab the needed plants that were standing by waiting to enrich the color scheme.

Visiting these gardens in person, or seeing them in glossy

magazines, is inspiring but a bit overwhelming. Walking down the center of a manicured green lawn flanked by twin colorful borders is pure paradise, but how can we create such heaven in our own gardens without feeling burdened by the time required to clip hedges, stake delphiniums, and cut off spent flowers?

Thinking about maintenance needs before choosing your plants will help. Properly constructed fences and walls will need less tending than formal hedges. Informal shrub borders can serve as backdrops for perennials and annuals with less pruning than clipped yew. Mixed borders using shrubs, perennials, and annuals can be interesting and will need less grooming than borders made strictly of perennials. When choosing plants, concentrate on those offering long bloom periods and good leaves. If you're short on time, avoid perennials like Pacific hybrid delphinium that must be staked carefully, and choose self-supporting perennials such as long-leaf veronica (*Veronica longifolia*), instead.

Whenever possible plant cleverly so that your plants can lean on each other. Lavender or dwarf boxwood hedges on the forward edge of a border are sturdy supports for rangy pink evening primrose (*Oenethera speciosa*) or floppy spiderwort (*Tradescantia virginiana*). Pea sticks, or the twiggy prunings from fruit trees and other woody shrubs, can be used as informal staking. Stuck carefully in the ground around the emerging shoots of peonies or chrysanthemums or other loose-growing, leggy perennials, the pea stakes will support the perennials subtly, without being conspicuous. By the time the plants have grown up and flowered, the stakes will have disappeared into the lower foliage. This kind of staking must be done early in the season to allow the plant time to grow up over the buttress. Worth the foresight and effort, this kind of staking is a great improvement over the alternative ramrod stake-and-tie method that makes perennial borders look like lumberyard displays.

To make your work easier, allow room at the back and front of your border for maintenance. Three feet between a hedge or wall and border is barely enough to get in and prune the hedge, train climbers onto the wall, or tend to the plants at the back of the border. Maintenance from the front of the border will be easier if you have a sidewalk or paving stones there to let the inevitably sprawling plants on the forward edge drape and spill. This will also make it easier to mow any lawn that you might have in front of the border. Another option is choosing upright, tidy edging plants or a low hedge to serve as your border's frame.

If your border is very deep, stepping-stones or paths cutting through diagonally can help you get to the middle and back to groom, divide, mulch, and fertilize plants when necessary. I've always enjoyed telling visitors with a straight face that I get into my twenty-foot-deep mixed border by walking on my hands, but even I have succumbed to necessity and made occasional paths to the jungle's interior. This also cuts down on soil compaction that results from regular trampling of beds and borders.

If they [gardeners] had developed naturally they . . . would have wings . . . so that they might float over the beds. Those who have had no experience cannot imagine how one's legs are in the way, when there is nothing to stand on . . . how impossibly short they are if one has to reach to the other side of the bed without treading on a clump of pyrethrum or on the shoots of columbine. If only one can hang in a belt and swim over the beds, or at least have four hands, with only a head . . . or have limbs telescoping like a photographic stand.

—Karel Capek
The Gardener's Year

The deeper your border, the more complex and rich your composition can be. I created a 20' deep × 50' long mixed border of trees, shrubs, perennials, bulbs, vines, and annuals to serve as a screen between my house and the road and to provide nearly-year-round color to enjoy from inside the house and from the street. This cuts down on mowing—my least favorite gardening chore—although it increases the amount of weeding and dead-heading. For many gardeners, this might be more work than desirable, and a narrower, shorter border with fewer plants might be more suitable. To make my work a bit easier, I mulch heavily to keep moisture in and weeds out, and plant tightly, leaving less room for weeds to invade.

Creating a border means juggling several balls in the air simultaneously. Plant height, spread, color, foliage, and season of bloom must all be orchestrated to form a symphony of ongoing color combinations. Heights of plants are generally low, medium, and tall from front to back of the border, although gardeners soon learn to break this rule often enough to avoid the look of a stair-case. Occasional tall but see-through plants such as *Gaura lindheimerii*, fisherman's wands (*Dierama pulcherrimum*), or *Verbena bonariensis*, placed in front and mid-border, help keep the progression of heights unpredictably interesting.

To think about heights on paper, it helps to divide the border artificially into front, middle and back as a reminder to keep the plants generally with the tallest ones to the back. To avoid an overly scattered look, concentrate your spring bloomers in one area, fall in another place, and summer in a third space. That way your color combinations will be strong in each area during one season, rather than dotted all around the border—chords here and there, rather than single notes. Even easier, if you are a beginner, make a one-season border and let it really shine during the time of year that you're most likely to see it. A winter border near the entry, a summer border by the back patio, and a spring border beside the driveway can give you three separate seasonal displays without the added complexity of combining them into one. This can also allow you three different color schemes to play with.

In a three- or four-season border, you can keep to one color scheme for all four seasons or use a different one for each season. After all, the plants are sequential in their blooming. This more complex task asks you to place your plants with overall thought to compatible heights and leaves, and also to remember to group them here and there for strong seasonal compositions in harmonious color.

Massing your plants in groups of three, five, or seven will make a greater impact than mixing individual plants. Think about the shapes of color that you want to result, and arrange your plants accordingly. Gertrude Jekyll, that masterful designer of perennial borders, set drifts of perennials diagonally into her borders, letting the color snake through at oblique angles. This way, when the bloom cycle ends, there isn't such an obvious gap in the color scheme. After all, you don't want a checkerboard. Think of a watercolor or tapestry and try to make your plants suggest that impression. Not that plants follow our orders, in any case; they weave and wander, lacing together and scrambling over each other, running underground and seeding around. Every gardener can tell you about a winning combination that happened by chance— a seedling with a mind of its own landing in just the right place. We contribute to the plan, and so does nature.

Plants grow at different rates. Rapidly spreading perennials such as yarrow and bearded iris are fine in a big border where space is ample, but overly domineering if planted with slower-growing perennials. For fairness, let the strong growers spread themselves out in larger borders, and plant the shyer clumping plants in smaller beds. Otherwise the rompers will elbow out the choice, small beauties.

Edging plants are the picture's frame and should be chosen for their foliage value. Like the ribbon on a package, they form a fine finishing touch. Seen close up in greatest detail, they must look attractive for most of the year. Next to a lawn, be sure to choose edging plants tall enough to contrast with the low grass. Perennials with grassy leaves, such as thrift or chives, blend right into the lawn visually, so choose larger leaves for contrast. Also, grassy weeds have a habit of seeding into grassy-looking perennials at the front of the border, camouflaging themselves too well. Some of the best edging plants have bold, rounded leaves. Lady's mantle (*Alchemilla mollis*) with lobed leaves that sparkle with morning dew, and sprays of delicate yellow-green flowers that bloom for six weeks in late spring, and again in summer if cut back after blooming, is a good choice. *Geranium renardii* with rounded leaves and charming white flowers penciled with violet lines makes a lovely accent at the front of the border. So do the marbled, round leaves of coral bells (*Heuchera* 'Bressingham Hybrids'), the divided dark green leaves of pink-flowering *Geranium sanguineum* 'Striatum' and white-flowering *Geranium sanguineum* 'Album.' Where there is enough room for draping, sprawling plants, grow the long-flowering *Potentialla* 'Rot' with silvery strawberrylike leaves and deep red flowers, or *Geranium riversleaianum* 'Mavis Simpson' with gray-green leaves and prolific silvery-pink flowers. Bloodroot (*Sanguinaria canadensis*), hosta, epimedium, rodgersia, astrantia and 'Palace Purple' coral bells must be grown at the front of the shade border. Their bold, beautiful leaves deserve close-up appreciation.

For mid-border, choose long-blooming perennials with big enough flowers, blooming high enough on the plant to be visible above the front edging plants. This is the place for the medium-height peonies, daylilies, yarrows, bellflowers, veronicas, and summer phloxes. Here you can get away with mediocre foliage, as the front edge will bear the brunt of responsibility for leaf excellence. Daylily flowers catch the eye in mid-border while their mediocre leaves are overlooked if succulent 'Autumn Joy' sedum stands in front of them. Powdery mildew on summer phlox or bee-balm leaves goes unnoticed hidden behind a froth of silvery 'Powys Castle' artemisia, while their showy flowers glow against the gray.

The large trumpets of Aurelian and Oriental lilies, the flat plates of 'Moonshine' and 'Coronation Gold' yarrow, and the billowing three-foot-wide bushes of *Aster frikartii's* blue daisies give ample color for mid-border. Spires of lavender-pink foxgloves and blue speedwell belong here as well for vertical accents. The shorter forms of Siberian iris—blue 'Ego' or 'Eric the Red,' for example—can be planted in mid-border. Save the taller blue 'Jaybird' and purple 'Caesar's Brother' for the back part of the border. Dusty-rose and white coneflowers (*Echinacea*), yellow threadleaf tickweed (*Coreopsis verticillata*), and black-eyed Susan (*Rudbeckia* 'Goldsturm') are all at home in mid-border. Milky bellflower (*Campanula lactiflora*), with its cloud of light-blue flowers topping the plant also belongs in the middle where it can lean companionably against its neighbors. The Armeniun geranium (*Geranium psilostemon*) with black-centered magenta flowers can settle its skirts on a crinoline of pea stakes in mid-border and no one will be the wiser.

The middle of the border is a good place to tuck the tall bulbs that flower at the tops of narrow stems. Alone they would be gawky giraffes, but planted to the sides or behind lower-growing plants, they blend into the picture harmoniously. Put red-flowering *'Lucifer' crocosmia* to the sides of blue *Aster frikartii* and let its stems arch and lean against the aster. Grow lily trumpets or globes of flowering onions (*Allium*) against clouds of meadow rue (*Thalictrum*) or behind silvery filigrees of *Artemisia canescens*, or *Artemisia* 'Lambrook Silver.'

Medium-height perennials tend to flower in summer, just as taller perennials are more likely to bloom in late summer or fall. One tactic to keep the tallest fall-flowering perennials from toppling without staking them is to cut them back to 1' tall in June, forcing them to branch more from the base and grow stockier and sturdier. This works well with Michaelmas daisies and sneezeweeds (*Helenium autumnale*). The leggy boltonia is now available in a more compact variety—'Snowbank'—and its lovely white daisies nicely accompany the pink, blue, and purple Michaelmas daisies.

August-blooming joe-pye weed (*Eupatorium purpureum*) towers at the back of the border on sturdy seven-foot stems, and its less gangly five-foot cousin, *Eupatorium purpureum* 'Atropurpureum' is a better height for most borders. Plume poppy (*Macleaya*) with blue-green leaves is a welcome back-border plant that is equally beautiful seen closer up. The plumy pink flowers of queen of the prairie (*Filipendula rubra*) are better seen from the back of the border, as the basal leaves, beautiful in spring, get quite shabby by summer. Tree mallow (*Lavatera thuringiaca*) and butterfly bush (*Buddleia davidii*) are excellent shrubby plants for back of the border; both flower all summer long. Tree-mallow flowers look as if hundreds of pink butterflies have landed all over the plant, while butterfly bush has thick, long columns of fragrant purple, pink or white flowers that indeed attract real butterflies.

For the narrower bed in a small garden, divide the border into two sections instead of three—back and front—and let the plants be equivalent in height to middle and front of a bigger border. Where space is limited, grow bulbs through perennials to get an added layer of color, and thread vines through and over shrubs. If you can't expand outward, plant deeper and send your plants higher, or experiment with layers of bulbs that bloom at different seasons, yet occupy the same patch of ground at different levels. Crocus planted 1" deep can mix easily with lilies buried 8" below ground and shallow-rooted perennials or annuals.

· ISLAND BEDS ·

Island beds are freestanding areas floating in a sea of lawn or paved surface. They have less structure than a border, which is crisply defined by an accompanying wall, hedge or fence, and can look a bit lost, like a stage without a backdrop. A strongly structured focal point within the island bed will help immensely. I have come to rely on three- to four-foot-tall ceramic birdbaths to do the job. Their terra-cotta color enhances the plants, and their solidity anchors the bed. Filled with water, their reflectivity adds interest, and visiting birds are a bonus. A sundial, tall urn, pot, or vertical piece of sculpture are equally effective.

Place an ornament of choice somewhere off center, a foot or two from the edge of the bed where it can be seen, yet also surrounded by plants on all sides, as if it, too, had grown out of the bed. Architectural plants placed toward the center of an island bed can also help ground the composition. The striking Griffith's spurge (*Euphorbia griffithii* 'Fireglow'), dramatic goat's beard (*Aruncus dioicus*), especially the cutleaf cultivar called 'Kneiffi,' and white loosestrife (*Lysimachia ephemerum*) are excellent specimen plants with upright form, interesting leaves, and unusual flowers. Try pur-

ple burnet (*Sanguisorba obtusa tenuifolia purpurea*) with its deep maroon bottlebrush flowers waving around at the top of its handsome
ferny leaves. If your island bed is big enough, a shrubby plant can
anchor the bed. Summersweet (*Clethra alnifolia*) is a good fragrant
plant for shade, 'Barnsley Pink' tree mallow a fine possibility in sun.

Proportion is everything in an island bed. The tallest plant
should be no higher than half the width of the bed. Stick with
slow- to moderate-growing plants and avoid the ones with gal-
loping habits, or your island bed will soon lose all balance. Grow
the plants with clumping growth habits and avoid the ones that
run rapidly underground, like gooseneck loosestrife (*Lysimachia
clethroides*). There is a place for overly aggressive plants—where
other plants won't grow, in dry shade or a wild garden—but not
in a contained island bed.

Because island beds are seen from all sides, tallest plants belong in the center, medium heights halfway toward the edge, and
shortest ones on the perimeter. It's important to select plants with
excellent leaves on the edge since they are seen close up and
frame the composition. Use several of one kind of plant on the
margin of the island bed for a well-defined line.

Since each island bed is a little world of its own, sticking to
a color scheme within each one will create unity. Several islands
are more effective than one. If you want them to relate well to
each other, repeat the colors and some of the same plants.

Why plant island beds? To cut down on the amount of grass
to mow. To add color to your garden. To dress up a large expanse
of paved surface. To brighten up a shady area. To find places to
house your growing collection of plants and organize them into
pleasing compositions.

One major advantage of island beds over borders that are

backed by hedges or walls is their ease of maintenance and viewing. You have access to work and look from all sides. Round ones
lend themselves easily to soaker hoses which can be laid out in
the bed like a coil, starting in the center and spiraling around into
bigger and bigger circles toward the edge. Set up the hose in early spring, before the plants have become too tall.

Rectangular island beds can form temporary walls or screens
where you need them for summer and fall and can do without
them in winter. In my own garden, I created a screen between the
upper and lower back yard by planting a long, narrow rectangle
(20' long by 7' wide) of summer phlox, Michaelmas daisy, bronze
fennel, sneezeweed (*Helenium*), and boltonia. This effectively created an immediate five foot tall wall of summer and fall flowers
that hid the undeveloped back forty from sight during the growing season. It formed a clear boundary between cultivated garden
space and wilderness. Like shutting the door on a messy storage
room, this flower bed gave me greater peace in the garden until I
was ready to tackle the outlying area.

Island beds allow you to develop the garden at your own
pace as time and money allow. One gardener I met in England allowed herself one new island bed a year. Since her husband did
the soil preparation, he was quite grateful for her restraint! Another technique is to compost on the site of next year's island bed
during this growing season. By next spring the compost will have
broken down into lovely soil, and you can work it right into the
bed and plant. For fastest decomposition of garden debris to
finished compost, pile grass clippings, small leaves, and soft vegetable peeling, layering with soil, and keeping the pile damp.
Three or four feet of debris will compress down to about one foot
of finished compost.

Since island beds are individual modules, you can revise their arrangement, and divide and move plants, with no impact on the larger design of your garden. I love perennials for their infinite variety and admit that their ease of moving is one of their most endearing traits. Imagine digging up a tree or shrub every time you changed your mind. With perennials it's easier than moving the furniture.

· MODIFIED BORDERS ·

It is not how much we have, but how much we enjoy, that makes happiness.
—Charles Spurgeon

Not everyone has room or gardening time for a big border. Often, though, we inherit a garden with plants scattered about randomly, as if someone had gone on a plant-buying binge, come home, and run around the yard digging holes and planting like a squirrel burying acorns. To make a composition out of these isolated plants, we can sometimes move them into a group or unite them by adding other shrubs and perennials to create a harmonious whole. This is the same as organizing furniture into seating arrangements instead of sticking chairs, tables, and lamps anywhere in the room. Plants form associations with each other and, after growing beside each other for a while, begin to look as if they belong together in a comfortable grouping.

A lone flowering plum tree in my garden became a modified island bed when sculptor Katy Mcfadden-Benecki placed her *Sleeping Gardener* at the base of the tree. The lawn beneath him died, and I took out enough grass around him to make a circle beneath the tree out to the drip line. Drought-tolerant, shade-loving perennials were planted; bishop's hat (*Epimedium*) and sweet wood-ruff, with a drift of 'Apricot Beauty' tulips to welcome spring. A few clumps of Labrador violet (*Viola labradorica purpurea*) were added because their dark purple leaves relate well to the dark brown earth tones of the sculpture, and their purple flowers bloom well into the summer.

Two isolated old fruit trees with root systems that defeated the lawn became the start of another island bed. Poor soil in this area required amending with compost, and tough plants were chosen, for the trees would surely continue to hog the water. Old roses proved to be good survivors, along with hardy geraniums, yellow loosestrife (*Lysimachia punctata*) and fall-flowering sedum (*Sedum spectabile*). To dress up the homely fruit trees, I threw a clematis up one and a climbing rose up another, carefully digging ample planting holes with plenty of compost added. Someday I will take out those ugly trees and start over, but meanwhile I have an adequate bed where I once had lone trees and dying grass.

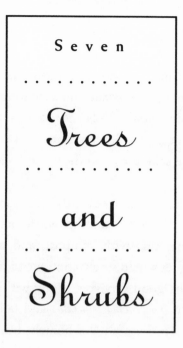

Seven

Trees

and

Shrubs

The ability to simplify means to eliminate the

unnecessary so that the necessary may speak.

—Hans Hofman

Search for the Real

. . .

When I first moved to my second garden, there were trees scattered everywhere, helter-skelter. An old gnarled weeping willow and a gargantuan columnar blue spruce dominated the front yard, dwarfing the modest one-story house. A forty-foot-tall sweet gum tree towered above the house in the backyard, along with a huge deodar cedar to the side. Fruit trees were growing here and there

with no rhyme or reason—a young hawthorn looking like a lol-
lipop was stuck in the middle of the lawn. It looked as if a meteor
shower of trees had landed and planted themselves. I could see
that the tree services were going to love me.

Unless I were planning to make my house taller, some of
these two-story trees had to go. For my home and garden to look
united, the trees and house must be in scale, or in good proportion to each other. My small house looks best with trees fifteen to
twenty-five feet tall. A taller two- or three-story house is a much
better candidate for forty-foot sweet gums, spruces, and cedars. If
only I could have transplanted these big trees to the newly built
dream homes that needed them!

When I took out the weeping willow and the pencil-shaped
spruce, the front yard came back to life, cleared of clutter. I
thought for a long time about what I wanted before choosing new
trees, and was careful about where I put them. Smart placement is
the key to living happily with trees. The very same kind of willow
that hogged the small space in my front garden looks magnificent
beside a creek in my neighbor's backyard.

· FORM ·

Before you choose a tree, find out how tall it will grow and how
wide it will spread. Then make sure that you give it a home where
it can grow freely to develop into its mature shape. Most of us fall
in love with trees when they flower and want them for their exciting color, but bloom time is usually a fleeting few weeks. For
most of the year, a tree is a shape in the garden; form gives a tree
its essential character.

When you look at a tree, if you squint you will see its form.

There are seven main crown shapes: ovate (egg-shaped), globe-shaped (round-headed), vase-shaped (diagonally spreading), weeping (pendant), pyramidal (cone-shaped), columnar (upright), and horizontal. Each of these forms is useful in the right place.

Columnar trees work well in a narrow, tall space against a two-story home on a small lot. A group of Armstrong maples (*Acer rubrum* 'Armstrong') that grow forty feet tall but only six feet wide make a strong vertical statement without taking up much room. In the fall their leaves turn brilliant red-orange. Amanogawa flowering cherry (*Prunus serrulata* 'Amanogawa') grows upright to twenty-five feet tall and offers pink flowers in spring. Use these columnar trees against a high wall—situated out in the open, they will look like lost giraffes on the veldt.

Weeping willows and cherries are lovely beside water, with their trailing branches leading your eye to a flowing creek, the grace and motion of plant and water enhancing each other. A small weeping laceleaf maple planted at the edge of a pool points to the water and has its beauty doubled in the pool's mirror. I've often seen this sculptural tree placed poorly in the middle of a lawn or cramped beside a doorway. It can spread ten feet across with age, and is best planted on a bank, berm, or above water, where its branching pattern can be thoroughly appreciated in all seasons.

Ovate (egg-shaped) trees and globe-shaped (round-headed) trees are similar in profile, generally rounded, with the ovate crowns somewhat narrower. These are graceful shapes for backdrop, specimen, or shade trees. The showy 'Rustica Rubra' saucer magnolia (*Magnolia soulangiana* 'Rustica Rubra') with its wide, large, rounded canopy spreading thirty feet across, is a popular specimen tree. Its promising furry buds release large, fragrant, satiny flowers, rose-red on the outside, white inside. Flowering on bare branches, it heralds spring with saturated color. Hybrid magnolia 'Galaxy' is ovate in shape, about twenty feet tall and twelve feet wide, with rich pink flowers. Its more slender profile is useful in a narrow space.

I am especially fond of moderately vase-shaped trees. Their graceful branches reach diagonally upward like dancing arms, leading the eye to nearby shrubs. Some of the flowering cherries have this shape—the Yoshino oriental cherry (*Prunus* × *yedoensis* 'Akebono'), for example. Its pink flowers delicately decorate the bare-branched tree, and then the ground below it as the petals fall in early spring. Some of the Japanese maples are vase-shaped— 'Burgundy Lace', for example, with deeply cut dark burgundy foliage. I love to look at the branches of these vase-shaped trees in winter and faithfully prune inward-growing and crossing branches to keep their lines clean and open.

Spreading or horizontally shaped trees are useful where you want to repeat the line of a flat roof or where you want a low canopy. Sargent's crabapple (*Malus sargentii*), growing ten feet tall and spreading twenty feet wide, has this shape. It offers white spring flowers and small profuse red berries in fall. Mount Fuji flowering cherry (*Prunus serrulata* 'Shirotae') grows about fifteen feet tall and spreads twenty feet or more across, with clusters of semidouble white flowers dangling from the branches in spring. I've seen it planted in large numbers as a street tree in our China-town, blooming magnificently, and also as a single specimen framing a bed beneath it. Because it blooms on bare branches, its pure white flowers show to great advantage.

Pyramidal trees are effective against tall buildings, or planted as specimens in a suitably large landscape. The 'Fairmount' ginkgo, moderately cone-shaped, looks spectacular when its yellow fall color contrasts with a dark wall. There's a marvelous planting of ginkgos in downtown Portland in front of a dark gray stone church. Japanese umbrella pine (*Sciadopitys verticillata*) stands best alone as a strong green pyramidal focal point. Silvery-blue Koster's spruce (*Picea pungens* 'Koster') has the same striking shape.

· PROBLEMS TO AVOID ·

Every spring my European birch tree gets aphids that drip sticky honeydew all over the plants below. Because I value the tree's dappled shade, I have a tree service drench the ground with a preventive insecticide, but I certainly wouldn't choose this tree for my garden. In my climate, many of the crabapples are prone to diseases, and the Florida dogwoods have been suffering from anthracnose. Even though these are beautiful trees when healthy, I recommend that you select a disease-resistant kousa dogwood instead.

I once worked in an estate garden with a windbreak of poplars that some well-intentioned gardener no doubt planted for their rapid growth rate. Poplars, like silver maple and cottonwoods, grow quickly and explosively, shattering brittle wood and leaves all over the garden. If you garden in a trance, as I do, noisy trees are unnerving. So are blowers—someday I'll write an ode to the rake. In my own garden, a brittle sweet gum tree startles me with sudden branch litter, and bombards me on a windy day with its spiny fruits that look like medieval maces. Forget going barefoot in the grass around a sweet gum tree. Poplars and sweetgums are also notorious surface-rooters and creep insidiously into lawns and flower beds, drying out the ground and raising the surface.

Choose trees with deep roots if you want to garden nearby. Before you fall in love with a tree, ask an unbiased professional about its merits and problems. No tree is perfect, but here are some fine possibilities to consider, with good form, moderate growth rates, and few drawbacks. Because you will place and choose trees with more success if you first ask yourself what purpose you want the tree to serve, my discussion of trees is grouped by function.

· TREES FOR SHADE ·

Perfectly symmetrical pairs of small, heart-shaped leaves sit opposite each other on every branch of the katsura tree (*Cercidiphyllum japonicum*), creating a most satisfying pattern. Once I sat through an entire hour of slides showing katsura trees in every season, without a single yawn. Its early spring leaves are reddish bronze, turning deep blue-green in summer and yellow in fall. Katsura trees in maturity can be forty feet tall, so this is a moderately large shade tree for the home garden. Elegant beauty, lovely form, and seasonal change of its foliage color make katsura a unique tree. Male trees usually have single trunks with pyramidal crowns, while female trees will often have multiple trunks and round crowns.

I always stop to admire the silver-leaved box elder (*Acer negundo* 'Variegatum'). Its green leaves with creamy white margins give the tree a refreshing silvery appearance, especially welcome in the dog days of summer. This tree eventually becomes forty feet tall with a round crown. A cultivar named 'Flamingo' is reported to grow thirty-five feet tall with an ovate crown; its new leaves are green with strong pink tints.

Paperbark maple (*Acer griseum*) is most noticeable in winter, when its warm orange-brown peeling bark commands attention. Its leaf shape and slow growth rate add to its value as a small shade tree. Leaves are three-parted, each leaflet only about two inches long, giving the tree a delicate look and casting dappled shade. Red and orange fall foliage color add to the interest of this unusual tree that slowly becomes twenty feet tall with an ovately shaped crown.

Where you need a small shade tree near a patio or in a court-yard, the Japanese snowbell (*Styrax japonica*) is outstanding. Maturing slowly to a thirty-foot tree, with a crown that spreads even wider, this tree is attractive year-round. In April small bright-green tapered leaves angle upward at the tops of the branches, giving the tree an uplifted look. In June small white flowers bloom below the branches, creating a tiered effect: layers of green leafy branches alternating with layers of dangling white flowers. Small oval green fruit forms after flowering. This is a lovely tree to look up into when it blooms, so if you can place it at the top of a stair-case or on a bank, so much the better.

If you have enough room for a large shade tree, the Japanese zelkova (*Zelkova serrata*) is unsurpassable. This vigorously growing tree is gracefully vase-shaped and will reach fity feet or more in maturity.

Please remember that shade trees will do their job well enough to make it nearly impossible for you to grow grass beneath them, let alone mow near the trunk. If you must have a tree in the lawn, make a large circle around it to keep from damaging the trunk with the mower or weedeater. Better yet, grow your lawn out in the open and plant trees with shrubs and ground cover beneath for easier gardening.

· SPRING-FLOWERING TREES ·

While flowering trees can certainly double as shade trees and offer the filtered shade that allows you to grow a good selection of understory plants, they're usually chosen first for their exciting burst of color that may last only a few weeks. Is it worth the quick thrill? Yes and no. If that's all the tree can offer, think twice before you choose it. Often though, the same tree that flowers in spring will have interesting fall color, fruit, or a pleasing branching pattern.

Every winter I look for the first signs of spring in my garden: the buds of the blireiana plum making tiny dots of maroon all along the bare branches, just enough to create a purplish haze. I watch with great anticipation for the day when the buds open to turn the whole tree rosy-pink with semidouble flowers. This vision lights up the garden on gray March days, inspiring me to write poems and giving me the necessary cheer to prepare my taxes. Although its flowering period is a short few weeks, the blireiana plum also leafs out with burgundy leaves, has a gnarled trunk that I enjoy looking at, and casts the kind of dappled shade that's just right for a picnic table. Its graceful, low, spreading canopy frames the beds nearby, uniting them with its outstretched branches.

Most of the flowering plums mature to a twenty- or twenty-five-foot height, ideal for the smaller garden. 'Thundercloud' (*Prunus cerasifera* 'Thundercloud') with a strong rounded crown, flowering pink, also has burgundy leaves after the bloom period.

Flowering cherries are spectacular in bloom, heralding spring with pastel pink, white and even shocking pink flowers. Before I moved to my second garden, I told myself that cherries were too obviously pretty, and that I would show good taste by choosing a more subtly beautiful tree. I changed my mind after moving to two-thirds of an acre, complete with trees, including a

'Shirofugen' flowering cherry that I thoroughly enjoy from my office window. I love the winter form of this tree, with its dark, definitive branches leaning diagonally like outstretched arms. I prune out any branches growing toward the center of the tree to keep its framework open and clean. In mid-spring reddish-brown leaves begin unfurling, echoing the burgundy leaves of the near-by blireiana plum. Later in spring, dark pink flower buds appear at the ends of long suspended stalks, soon to open and bloom pink. This twenty-foot tree branches low on the trunk, making it an ideal screening plant. Although it has some surface roots, it's easy to find pockets of soil in between where you can plant low-growing hardy geraniums and daylilies for later color.

With so many flowering cherries to choose from, you can narrow down the field by deciding on the form that best fits your garden: spreading, weeping, vase-shaped, or globe-shaped. Do you prefer single, double or semidouble flowers? Single flowers look like apple blossoms, with one layer of petals around the center, while double flowers have many more petals, giving them a thicker look. Some cherries offer flowers before leafing out, showing off their color that much more on bare branches. For that quality, and the grace of their branching pattern, I love the light pink Yoshino oriental cherry (*Prunus* × *yedoensis*) and the pink 'Daybreak' cherry (*Prunus yedoensis* 'Akebono') Several of these flowering cherries poised on a hillside in our Japanese garden make an ethereal sight.

I fell in love with the Yulan magnolia (*Magnolia denudata*) the first time I saw its luminous, ivory-white, tulip-shaped flowers standing above the dark bare branches like candles against the spring sky. Because I could not find one, I chose the next best tree, the creamy-white version of the saucer magnolia, *Magnolia soulan-*

giana 'Lennei Alba.' It illuminates my front garden in early spring. If I had a bigger garden, I'd also plant the goddess magnolia (*Magnolia sprengeri* 'Diva') for its large bright-pink flowers. 'Royal Crown' magnolia with intense pink tapered buds that remind me of candle flames, opening to ten-inch flowers. Fortunately there are several wonderful magnolia collections close enough to home for me to visit, enjoy, and covet. The rich pink magnolia 'Caerhays Belle' is on my wish list after seeing it shown during a slide show.

For the smaller garden, 'Susan,' a magnolia with red-purple buds and deep-pink flowers is valuable for its compact globe-shaped form. 'Galaxy,' moderately ovate in shape, is also useful where space is restricted; its profuse flowers are a lovely deep pink. A spectacular garden that I visit as often as I can has deep-pink 'Galaxy' near pastel-pink Veitch magnolia in full view of the home's windows.

The showy magnolias do have a few drawbacks. Because they are surface rooting it's best not to garden beneath them. And though their sumptuous flowers are heavenly in spring, the leaves that follow are often coarse.

Spring color is enriched by the flowering crabapples, many of which also offer a good fall fruit display. Fungal diseases have given crabapples a bad reputation; so has their twiggy, dense growth habit. An informative article in *Fine Gardening* magazine by Dr. Thomas L. Green encourages us to write the International Ornamental Crabapple Society for information on disease-resistant crabapples suited to specific areas of the country (Dr. Green, Morton Arboretum, Lisle, IL 60532). Where I live, the Japanese crabapple (*Malus floribunda*) thrives, every branch covered with dark pink buds opening to creamy pink flowers, looking the color of strawberry-and-cream ice cream. I know it's April when the

Japanese crabapples decorate the hillsides with their wands of creamy pink. Their dense, twiggy crowns and fall fruit offer shelter and food for the birds.

When I had room for only one tree, in my first small garden, I chose the kousa dogwood (*Cornus kousa*). Growing twenty feet or more, with a moderately vase-shaped crown, kousa dogwood is often seen as a multistemmed tree. Its growth pattern met my need to shade the west side of my house and screen the living-room window from the road with a beautiful tree that bloomed later than the more common eastern and western dogwoods. Kousa dogwood is the most disease resistant of its genus and flowers longer, for three to four weeks in late spring and early summer. Its creamy-white flowering bracts bloom above the leaves, making repeating horizontal layers of green and white. This tree is especially beautiful when viewed from above, so consider it when you need a tree to look down upon from a deck or a second-story window. A fall bonus of strawberry-shaped fruit and dark red leaf color add value to this fine tree.

When I look for unusual trees and shrubs, I head for Richard Bush's nursery in Canby, Oregon. When I asked about his favorite kousa dogwood cultivars, Dick extolled the virtues of four: 'Moonbeam,' which boasts ten-inch flowers; 'Weaver's Weeping,' which cascades toward the ground; 'Bush's Pink,' with the same flower color as the pink eastern dogwood, and 'Snow Boy,' with white flowers and variegated leaves. He sent me off with a list of thirty-eight cultivars grown at his nursery, each unique in its size, shape, leaf color, and flower color.

The Stellar hybrid dogwoods, crosses of the eastern dogwood with the kousa dogwood, introduced recently by Dr. Elwin R. Orton, Jr. of Rutgers University, are promising new spring-blooming trees. Four are upright in form: 'Stellar Pink,' with rosy-pink flowering bracts, and three white hybrids named 'Constellation,' 'Galaxy,' and 'Aurora.' White Stellar hybrids 'Ruth Ellen' and 'Stardust' are broad and spreading. An article by the propagator in the March 1993 issue of *Fine Gardening* describes them in greater detail.

There is so much summer color from shrubs and perennials that summer-flowering trees are of less consequence. Should you need one, the ferny-leaved silk tree (*Albizzia julibrissin*) makes a lovely specimen or small shade tree. Its spreading vase-shaped canopy is topped with fluffy fragrant pink flowers that are especially beautiful seen from a deck or second-story window.

Three delightful, fragrant magnolias that flower in summer are suitable for the smaller garden—the oyama magnolia (*Magnolia sieboldii*), Wilson magnolia (*Magnolia wilsonii*), and Watson magnolia (*Magnolia watsonii*). These small, spreading trees have pendant white flowers decorated with red stamens. Since the flowers dangle below the leaves they are seen to best advantage at the top of a slope. As they bloom after the trees have leafed out, don't expect them to offer the drama that the spring magnolias deliver when they flower on bare branches.

· TREES FOR FALL ·

Beauty in the fall garden can vie easily with the mainly pastel glory of the spring garden. Autumn brings a warmer palette, with brilliant red, red-orange, and yellow foliage and fruit. Fall's beauty is poignant, reminding us that its blaze of color is the last surge before winter takes hold. Although winter has its own appeal,

most gardeners simply feel strange without dirt under their finger-
nails. Digging and raking, weeding and deadheading are chores
that ground me in a way that no winter activity does.

Fall flowers are especially welcome because they are late in
the sequence of bloom and scarcer than summer's bounty. Harle-
quin glorybower (*Clerodendrum trichotomum*) is a round-headed tree
that grows twenty feet tall. Rub the fuzzy leaves and you will get
a whiff of peanut butter. The white flowers that begin to open in
August are delightfully fragrant, and when the petals drop, red-
dish-maroon calyces hang on. When shiny turquoise fruits form
at the center of the calyces, they look like jeweled beads surrounded by maroon stars. When the leaves fall, all these red and
turquoise ornaments sparkle against the bare branches.

Maples, oaks, and sweet gums are spectacular in fall but need
to be chosen carefully, keeping in mind their ultimate size and
shape. For the most part, these trees have big leaves, casting
dense shade and dropping significant litter, so be aware of these
traits before you decide. For the best fall foliage color, choose
your tree in autumn, since individual trees within the same species
will have quite a range of tints. Most trees will color up more intensely in sun than in shade.

If your garden is small, consider the slow-growing Japanese
maples (*Acer palmatum*) for fall color. These graceful, spreading
vase-shaped trees with multiple trunks and delicately indented
leaves make excellent focal points in the garden. Green-leaved
trees offer the best red fall color. The Amur maple (*Acer ginnala*) is
another small multitrunked tree with brilliant red fall color—it
grows quickly to about twenty feet tall and equally wide. 'Autumn
Flame' red maple (*Acer rubrum* 'Autumn Flame') is a thirty-five foot

tall, round-headed tree with early, dependable fall foliage color ranging from brilliant deep yellow to scarlet.

If you prefer the unusual, hunt down the fernleaf full-moon maple (*Acer japonicum* 'Aconitifolium'), also known as the dancing-peacock maple. Its deeply indented leaves, handsome in all seasons, are named for their similarity to monkshood. In spring clusters of small red flowers dangle, like delicate earrings from long stems below the bright green leaves. This tree comes into its glory with brilliant red foliage in the fall. Because it often has multiple trunks it can act as a screen; it also makes a fine specimen with all the interest of a strong piece of sculpture.

Although thorny and densely branched, hawthorn trees do offer valuable fall color. Their red-orange fruit draws grosbeaks and woodpeckers, and their twiggy, crossing branches offer shelter for birds and squirrels. The most common English hawthorns serve best as hedgerows on the periphery of a larger garden. For more graceful features in the smaller garden, choose one of the round-headed varieties with colorful red fruit. Carriere hawthorn (*Crataegus lavallei*) is the least twiggy, with an open branching structure, dark green leaves that turn bronzy-red and large orange-red fruit that remain through the winter. Washington hawthorn (*Crataegus phaenopyrum*) has a graceful shape, shiny red fruit, and is most resistant to fireblight, a bacterial disease that makes flowering shoots wilt and look scorched. 'Autumn Glory' hawthorn has the largest glossy red fruit, but its twiggy, dense crown and susceptibility to fireblight are drawbacks.

If you are patient and have enough gardening years ahead of you, put the sourwood tree (*Oxydendrum arboreum*) at the top of your list for fall color. Slow-growing to a pyramidal twenty-five-foot tree, its fall color is brilliant red. Clusters of white flowers reminscent of andromeda bloom in late summer, and their seed capsules make silvery accents against the red fall foliage. Unusual and good-looking, this tree never fails to gain my admiration in fall.

Franklin tree (*Franklinia alatamaha*) is another unusual tree that takes my breath away in fall. Its leaves turn red at about the same time as its white, single, fragrant flowers open, creating quite a stir in the garden.

Stewartia mondelpha is another of my favorite fall color trees. It has a graceful, spreading canopy, rich orange-brown bark, and tapered leaves that turn orange and red in autumn. Small white flowers bloom surprisingly in late summer, when most of the garden is on the wane.

· WINTER TREES ·

Please remember to place your winter accents where you can best enjoy them: near the doorways, and in plain view from the windows. If you can't be outside in the garden, let the garden at least give you visual pleasure until you can once again tend it and touch it.

Winter flowers are rare and immeasurably welcome to tide us over during the season that's bleakest for the dedicated gardener. Witch hazel (*Hamamelis mollis*), with fragrant, ribbony yellow flowers adorning bare winter branches, forms a small spreading tree that will grow in sun or shade. 'Pallida' has the best light yellow flowers, while 'Diane,' a variety of *Hamamelis intermedia*, has dark red-orange flowers. Witch hazels show up best against a backdrop of dark conifers—Alaska yellow cedar (*Chamaecyparis nootkatensis*) for example. Cornelian cherry (*Cornus mas*), another small, spreading tree, takes on a misty yellow appearance in winter, when tiny yellow flowers cover its bare branches. A bonus of red cherrylike fruit decorates the tree in autumn, attracting the birds.

Bark provides winter interest—without their leaves, deciduous trees are more noticeable for their trunks and branching patterns. Ribbon-bark cherry (*Prunus serrula*) invites you to run your hand along its satiny smooth mahogany-red trunk—no one can resist. If you place this tree so that the afternoon sun backlights the bark, the color will glow.

It's hard not to peel back a length of the orange-brown bark of a paperbark maple's (*Acer griseum*) trunk to take home and admire. This excellent small pyramidal tree casts dappled shade and has red fall foliage. Although its three-part leaves look nothing like a maple, its showy winged seeds will remind you that indeed it is.

The striking white bark of Jaquemont's birch (*Betula utilis jacquemontii*) will brighten the drabbest winter garden. Strong white branches reach upward and outward to form an upright, ovate crown. This elegant tree makes a powerful focal point from a distance, beckoning the viewer to approach for a closer look. Yellow fall leaf color adds to its beauty.

Coral-bark maple (*Acer palmatum* 'Sangokaku') is a popular tree for winter and fall interest. Vibrant red bark warms the winter garden, and yellow fall leaf color illuminates the picture in fall. This small tree, growing twenty to twenty-five feet tall, has gracefully spreading branches and a moderately globe-shaped crown. I like to place it with other red-stemmed and red-leaved plants, close enough to echo the color, yet sufficiently far away to let the maple have the lead. The red-stemmed, variegated shrubby dogwood (*Cornus alba* 'Elegantissima'), dwarf cranberry bush (*Viburnum opulus nana*) and Japanese bloodgrass (*Imperata cylindrica* 'Rubra') are good candidates for supporting cast.

Needle evergreens make fine additions to the winter garden. I like firs best—their needles are soft to the touch and varied in color. White fir (*Abies concolor*) is actually blue-white with needles that curve upward gracefully. The variety 'Candicans' is a dazzling silvery-blue that lights up a winter garden. Korean fir (*Abies koreana*) is dark green with short, stiff, curved needles that are dark green above and silver beneath, making a lovely pattern. Its young cones are upright burgundy ornaments in springtime, turning dark blue-violet by summer. This tree, like many conifers, has a pyramidal shape, growing slowly to thirty feet.

The handsome Hinoki false cypress (*Chamaecyparis obtusa*) is a moderately sized conifer with a lot of movement: the way its branches are layered creates a dynamic swirling effect. Cripps golden false cypress (*Chamaecyparis obtusa crippsii*) is a cultivar prized by lovers of yellow foliage, but is not my cup of tea. When it comes to conifers I'm happier with greens, blue-greens and bronze tones. I especially love interesting textures. The Japanese cedars (*Cryptomeria*) intrigue me, especially the feathery reddish-brown plume cedar (*Cryptomeria japonica* 'Elegans') and the stiffly braided 'Spiralis' cryptomeria. Umbrella pine (*Sciadopitys verticillata*) delights me—its bright-green needles are whorled around the stem like spokes. Look up the stem and you will see hundreds of miniature palm trees. Place the umbrella pine by itself, where you will best appreciate its symmetrical pyramidal shape.

Bristlecone pine (*Pinus aristata*) has dark needles coated with white resin. It grows slowly with an interesting irregular form that can give a feeling of age to a young, small garden. Japanese black

Before: This bed containing a mature birch tree had some problems: dry soil due to the birch roots, and a steep drop that made gardening awkward. This bed stands between my garden and my neighbor's driveway, where a large white motor home is parked, detracting from the garden's beauty.

After: Being careful not to change the level of the ground near the birch tree, I filled the bed elsewhere with rocks, followed by manure and compost, to reduce the steep pitch. To screen the neighboring driveway and motor home, I planted an informal hedge of drought-tolerant rugosa roses at the back of the bed— 'Grootendorst Pink', 'Conrad F. Meyer', and 'Blanc Double de Couvert'. These roses flower repeatedly during the summer. I added more drought-tolerant old roses to the middle of the bed, along with tall yellow mulleins (*Verbascum*). A hedge of fragrant 'Grosso' lavender edges the front of the bed, blooming all summer.

Before: This narrow bed in the shade of a two-story home faces a swimming pool used all summer. The first time I saw it, two large Japanese aralias (*Fatsia japonica*) filled the bed, blocking all light to the windows and obscuring the view out. Once these shrubs were removed, I was able to plant shade-loving shrubs and perrenials which bloom all summer yet stay well below the windows.

After: I chose pink mop-head hydrangeas for their round, showy flowers and *Astilbe tacquetii* 'Superba', with upright, lavender-pink plumes, for contrast. Hardy, upright fuschias with delicate tubular flowers fill the gaps, while Carpathian harebell (*Campanula carpatica*) drapes its blue flowers onto the sidewalk.

Before: When I first saw this raised bed with a mature red, laceleaf Japanese maple and one red rosebush, I thought of removing the rose and creating a quiet Japanese-style garden with subtle colors and textures. The owners vetoed this idea, asking for stronger, year-round color that they could enjoy from both the nearby patio and the house.

After: For this hot, dry raised bed, I chose drought-tolerant herbs, spurges, and sedums to maximize year-round foliage color and texture. Although none of these plants suggest the Japanese style that I first had in mind, their colors and textures are compatible with the laceleaf maple, and they satisfied the homeowners' needs. Annual white sweet alyssum provides fragrance and helps soften the harsh pavement while gray santolina, variegated sedum (*Sedum alboroseum* 'Variegatum') and *Sedum spectabile* contribute foliage and flower color.

Before: Spring, 1989. This large, sunny space at the southern end of my garden will become the picture seen from my office windows, from the grape arbor benches, and from the main path leading down the back yard. The larger-than-life-size sculpture entitled "Sunbathers" —a high-fired ceramic work by Katy McFadden-Benecki—has been placed as a focal point at the front of this border.

After: June, 1993. To allow access for gardening and strolling, the space has been divided into two beds with a path between them which cannot be seen by the head-on viewer. Because this border is visible from so many points of view, long-blooming hybrid musk roses, English roses, and perennials have been planted to provide color from June through October. Hybrid musk rose 'Mozart', with deep pink-red flowers, flourishes behind the "Sunbathers", while a hedge of light yellow *Coreopsis* 'Moonbeam' and deep pink Sweet William flower at their feet. Queen-of-the-meadow (*Filipendula ulmaria*) makes a cream-colored accent in the distance.

Before: When the "Sleeping Gardener", a ceramic sculpture by Katy McFadden-Benecki, first came to rest under this dwarf plum tree, his only company was a group of nearby 'Apricot Beauty' tulips and Ringo the cat. Mowing grass near this sculpture was impossible, so an island bed was designed around the piece.

After: I added ground covers that could tolerate shade and drought, for the roots of the plum tree rob the soil of most water, while its low canopy casts shade. I chose subtle plants with good leaves so that the sculpture would dominate the composition: white-flowering sweet woodruff, purple *Viola labradorica* and bishop's hat (*Epimedium*) with heart-shaped leaves and yellow spring flowers. (This bed is discussed in the chapter on beds and borders under 'Modified Borders.')

Before: Because my house faces a busy road and neighboring houses, I wanted screening for privacy, and colorful shrubs and perennials to enjoy from my windows. I favored deciduous plants over evergreens to maximize flower color and light.

After: Grown-up, mixed border nearly obscures the neighbor's house and the road. Trees and shrubs include winter-blooming 'Dawn' viburnum, spring-flowering 'Lennei Alba' saucer magnolia, dwarf Meyer's lilac, early-summer-blooming mock orange, and *Rosa glauca*. Tall blue speedwell (*Veronica longifolia*), pink cranesbill (*Geranium endressii*), white *Guara lindheimerii* and yellow lady's mantle (*Alchemilla mollis*) add summer color and texture. (This border is discussed in the chapter on beds and borders.)

Before: An arch with attached benches has been added to existing grape arbor for shaded seating and to support climbing roses and honeysuckle.

After: Visitors stop to rest and view the south end of the garden from these benches. Climbing rose 'New Dawn' flowers in light pink and scents the air, along with several honeysuckles. (The grape arbor is discussed in the chapter on garden structures.)

Before: A purple-leaved plum tree (*Prunus blireiana*) and flowering cherry are the main focal points in my back yard, which is mainly lawn. A large patch of bare ground left from the previous owner's trailer home suggested a place for an island bed. And since I hate to mow and love to garden, three island beds seemed like an even better idea.

After: I designed these island beds for the maximum amount of spring and summer color, using perennials with long bloom periods and interesting leaves. Ceramic bird baths by Cynthia Spencer help anchor the compositions. The grape arbor, a strong structural element, can be seen in the distance. Some long-blooming perennials chosen for the island beds are yellow *Coreopsis* 'Moonbeam', blue speedwell (*Veronica longifolia*), pastel pink *Geranium sanguineum* 'Striatum' and hot pink moss campion (*Lychnis coronaria*). Gray-leaved *Artemesia pontica* and *Artemesia* 'Powys Castle' add the foliage interest.

pine (*Pinus thunbergiana*) can easily be pruned to expose its asymmetrical branching pattern. It too gives a sense of maturity to the garden.

· TREES AS SCULPTURE ·

Gnarled trunks that lean, branches that zigzag or weep, contorted or layered structure give trees character. Recently consulting in an unusual garden, I noticed the owner's preference for structure through architectural plants with strong lines that were asymmetrical and complex. Her fondness for mature Japanese laceleaf maples with gnarled branches that are most visible in winter started us thinking about trees as sculpture in the garden.

Once I become aware of a concept, it seems that I see it exemplified everywhere. For the next few weeks I began to see sculptural trees in every garden. The very next day I saw a magnificent old winter hazel (*Corylopsis spicata*) that had been pruned to ressemble a mature laceleaf maple by exposing the trunk and branches. It was a piece of sculpture in the winter garden, standing about five feet tall and spreading at least eight feet across.

Nearby a contorted filbert (*Corylus avellana* 'Contorta') with craggy, twisted branches stood ten feet tall and spread equally wide. Yellow catkins dangling from the branches shimmered in the winter sun. Taller yet, the zigzagging outline of weeping mulberry (*Morua alba* 'Pendula') invited our admiration. A neighboring garden won the prize for drama with an ancient architectural camperdown elm (*Ulmus glabra* 'Camperdownii') sited perfectly on a slope. We looked up and marveled at its amazing weeping branches that spread and zigzagged toward the ground. I could easily imagine a dark stormy night with lightning flashes illuminating this gothic tree.

'Royal Purple' smoke tree (*Cotinus coggygria* 'Royal Purple') is one of my favorite small trees. I love its reddish-purple leaves, its adaptability to shade or sun, and the way it forms a wide, spreading shape. With selective pruning I turn it into a piece of living sculpture and enjoy its form and foliage against the north wall of my house.

I saw my first pagoda tree (*Cornus alternifolia* 'Argentea') from the window of a garden tour bus in Connecticut and couldn't wait to rush off and make a beeline for the tree. I was completely smitten by its creamy variegated leaves and striking form; layers of branches sit on the horizontal plane like so many tiers stepping down to ground level. The light-colored foliage shines like a beacon and has a cooling effect on the summer garden.

· GROVES ·

If you are blessed with an already existing grove of trees, you have the backbone for a woodland garden. An underplanting of shade-loving shrubs and ground covers will complete the picture. If you wish to create a grove, trees with small leaves and open branching will give you dappled shade, allowing you favorable light for growing a large range of understory plants.

Van Dusen Gardens in the heart of Vancouver, British Columbia, has a lovely grove of birches underplanted with drifts of heaths and heathers. In winter the white trunks of the birches combine well with the bronze and green tints of the heaths and heathers. Paperbark birch (*Betula papyrifera*) with creamy white bark that peels off in layers is especially striking. Imagine the white trunks in spring with pools of pink creeping phlox (*Phlox subulata*) and drifts of lavender aubretia (*Aubretia deltoides*).

I remember a golden grove of quaking aspen (*Populus tremuloides*) glistening in the sun against blue sky on a fall day in Montana. Their smooth gray-white trunks add winter appeal. Aspens do best at higher elevations; they are native to the western mountains. A group of ginkgo trees can provide similar brilliant fall color at lower altitudes. Their open, irregular branches and small fan-shaped leaves add an exotic look to the garden.

Serviceberry (*Amelanchier laevis*) with small leaves, white spring flowers, bird-attracting dark blue fruits and yellow and red fall foliage color, is an excellent small tree for groves. Underplant with lingonberry (*Vaccinium vitis-idaea*) and you will have a red fruit crop, too, suitable for making delicious tart jelly.

Japanese maples and vine maples (*Acer circinatum*) lend themselves to groves. Vine maples are often used as understory trees in shade, but they color up best in fall in full sun. Both of these maples benefit from pruning to keep their branching structure clean.

To space your trees for a grove, play around with stakes in the ground until you get a loose, informal pattern. Don't line your trees up like soldiers unless you want your grove to look like an orchard.

· SHRUBS FOR THE GARDEN ·

How difficult it would be to compose a satisfactory garden

without shrubs. Apart from the interest and beauty of their flowers, berries and leaves, their great contribution is the solidi-

ty which they add to the planting and design. They and they

alone are capable, if rightly placed, of dividing the garden into

separate areas and thus adding surprise to its many joys.

—*Graham Stuart Thomas*

Shrubs are living green garden walls. They separate your garden from adjacent properties and can also form partitions within your garden, separating the larger garden into garden rooms. They also serve as backbone to a border, thickening the plantings and adding texture, color, and form.

Shrubs are the great workhorses of the garden, growing quickly to give us walls, understory, backdrop, screening. I don't stop to admire the old privet hedge that separates me from my neighbor's huge white motor home, but I'm grateful that the previous owner of my house thought ahead and planted a green privacy screen on the property line, long before the neighbor's house was even built. Much as we like our neighbors, we might not share their enthusiasm for dogs, woodpiles, and sports. Having a basketball land in the middle of your favorite rosebush can be unnerving—even a small, innocent golf ball can shatter your garden reverie and break a cane full of flowers. Gardeners almost always live next door to more casual folks who like the natural look of blackberries, bamboo, and morning glory, blissfully oblivious to the menacing runners that race under the fence. There is simply no justice in a world where gardeners send canes of flowering roses over the fence, only to receive blackberry vines in exchange!

· SHRUBS AS WALLS: ·
BACKDROP AND SCREENING

Shrubs help stem the tide of weeds and basketballs; they block eyesores as well. If you have enough time to clip hedges, or enough money to hire someone to help you, dense evergreen walls of Canadian hemlock (*Tsuga canadensis*), arborvitae (*Thuja*), yew (*Taxus*), English holly (*Ilex aquifolium*) or incense cedar (*Calocedrus decurrens*) can give you total privacy. These are all relatively fine-textured plants that will provide a green backdrop without taking any attention away from your flowering perennials or shrubs.

Where I live there has been a terrible epidemic of photinia hedges. I get a headache looking at the shiny reddish brown new leaves in spring, and I'm sure the owners get other aches from the twice-yearly clipping required to keep these hedges from growing to the size of small trees. Laurel hedges are green at least, less violent in color but equally distracting with big, shiny leaves. They inevitably grow too tall and too wide for the home garden, with thick woody branches that beg for the chain saw. The litter they drop is also a gardener's nightmare: brown leathery leaves winter and spring, and hundreds of small black fruits that sprout in the flower beds.

I much prefer informal hedges of flowering shrubs. They need more room to spread than clipped hedges, but their flowers and fragrance give me far greater pleasure.

In my own garden I've made a thick screen of lilacs and shrub roses along the west property line. The lilacs bloom with purple, pink, and white fragrant flowers in April and May, lovely in the garden and delightful for cutting. They are barely done blooming when the roses begin flowering in late May. I have once-blooming old roses and repeat-flowering rugosa, bourbon, and hybrid musk roses. Foxgloves, mallows, asters, and penstemons add layers of extra color to the screen, filling in while the shrubs grow up. The lilacs began as suckering shoots from a friend's hedge—I grew them in two-gallon pots for a couple of years before planting them. This is a great way to keep plants growing until you figure out where you want to use them.

I like to tuck some fragrant mock orange (*Philadelphus coronarius*) into a big screening border. The scent of its white flowers in the garden or cut for the house is unsurpassable. As a plant, mock orange is leggy and twiggy, best pruned regularly and grown where it will fade into the backdrop, before and after it blooms. I've trained a 'Tetrarose' Montana clematis up the trunks of my mock orange to soften its bare-legged look. Mock orange is actually best placed on your neighbor's property, just behind a six-foot fence, which will support it while it drapes and spills into your garden. See if you can work that out with your neighbor!

The most breathtaking mock orange I've ever seen is 'Belle Etoile,' a medium-sized shrub filled with single white flowers with striking mauve centers. This and any number of other hybrid, compact mock oranges are useful in a mixed border. Pictures of the white-variegated form of mock orange, described as a fragrant, slow, compact shrub, look very appealing.

Driving on country roads in May, I have often seen old farmhouses with masses of purple and lavender lilacs flowering beside one or two snowball bushes, with their showy spheres of white flowers. This is the common snowball (*Viburnum opulus* 'Sterile') that can be used along with lilacs for screening. The closely related European cranberry bush (*Viburnum opulus*) is a similarly tall, deciduous shrub, with maplelike lobed leaves and white lacecap flowers that form red showy tart fruits for the fall garden. The

American cranberry bush (*Viburnum trilobum*) is very similar, but bears sweeter berries that are used for making preserves—if you get to them before the birds do.

My very favorite viburnum has strongly scented pink flowers in winter and early spring. 'Dawn' viburnum (*Viburnum bodnantense* 'Dawn') stands in the middle of my deep mixed border, underplanted with pink and white Lenten roses (*Helleborus orientalis*). 'Dawn' makes an equally good backdrop shrub and can serve as a small courtyard tree if trained to have only one trunk. I can see my own shrubby 'Dawn' viburnum from the kitchen window—it gets me through the bleak winter days. Handsome, oval green leaves with a pleated pattern turn red in the fall. Soon after they drop, flower buds appear that begin to bloom in the fall and continue into winter and early spring.

'Mariesii' doublefile viburnum (*Viburnum plicatum tomentosum* 'Mariesii') is a fine backdrop shrub, flowering with great flamboyance, even though it's white. Lys de Bray, in her *Manual of Old-fashioned Shrubs*, describes it perfectly: "It has tiers of branches from which stand up double rows of flower buds. The stems extend and the buds unfold until each branch is surmounted by flat, hydrangea-like creamy flowers clustered like a snowfall all along the top of each branch." Masses of these viburnums planted along a waterfront park in Portland would surely cause frequent traffic accidents if cars weren't moving as slowly as they are forced to along this congested road.

The evergreen andromeda (*Pieris japonica*) blooms in spring with clusters of pendant, scented, flowers that resemble lily-of-the-valley, as pretty in the bud stage as fully opened. Mature plants grow ten to twelve feet tall and make marvelous screens. Too often they are planted smack in front of a window where they obscure the view. Then they are pruned to open the view, and their graceful form is ruined. I suppose they look innocently petite in their nursery containers, and their small leaves belie their ultimate size. Where I live, andromeda will grow in sun or shade as long as it's watered, although most texts describe it as shade-loving. Pink, rose, and white flowering forms are yours to choose from. There is also a variegated form that is slower growing.

In shade, camellias and the taller rhododendrons are sturdy flowering plants for screening, and they are evergreen to boot. Twice I have moved to homes with huge rhododendrons planted right in front of picture windows. I had plenty of privacy, but no light. As soon as I could arrange it, I found new homes for these shrubs. Friends came equipped with shovels, crowbars, wheelbarrows, and trailers to dig out these tree-size shrubs and place them where they belong—in the distance, screening for privacy. I gleefully waved good-bye to my plants, happy that they were going to more suitable places, where they would serve their purpose and be better appreciated. It's so much easier to part with plants when you can recycle them to a welcoming garden.

If you're looking for big evergreen screening plants for shade, 'Loderi King George' is a majestic large-leaved rhododendron with pink buds opening to very fragrant flowers. It's quite sensational when it blooms in May. I discovered an unusually charming, tall, semidouble lavender rhododendron in my own garden and learned its name from a knowledgeable friend: 'Fastuosum Flore Pleno.' Someday, when I've learned all the roses, perennials, and clematis, I promise to join the Rhododendron Society, but it may be a while.

Often there's a place in the garden used mainly in summer that needs privacy. Butterfly bush (*Buddleia davidii*) is a wonderful

solution, easily growing six feet in its first year, eventually standing eight to ten feet tall. This deciduous shrub thrives on neglect,
is drought tolerant, puts up with heavy clay soil, and will grow in
abandoned railroad yards with no care. In my garden it is happiest in full sun and performs best if pruned down to two feet in the
spring. It rises up like a phoenix with large panicles of fragrant
flowers that attract butterflies. Purple, lavender, pink, white, blue-
lavender and rich violet-purple forms of butterfly bush are available. Although I love the white form when it flowers, I dislike the
brown color of its fading spikes and can never deadhead it quickly enough to keep the whole bush white.

'Pink Delight' butterfly bush flowering behind a bench at the
New York Botanical Garden with lavender 'Dropmore' catmint
(*Nepeta* × *faassenii* 'Dropmore') was a vision I will never forget. Sitting on that bench, inhaling the honey scent of buddleia and
watching the butterflies hover was perfect entertainment on a hot
August afternoon. 'Pink Delight' has extra-long spikes of clear
pink flowers, and is on my wish list. My favorite butterfly bush, so
far, is 'Lochinch,' a hybrid between *Buddleia fallowiana* and *Buddleia
davidii*, with especially gray foliage and profuse lavender flower
clusters. I love it beside pink tree mallow (*Lavatera thuringiaca*) with
some fragrant 'Pink Perfection' lilies thrown in for good measure.

This spring I'm building a screening bed to serve as a final
border and also to hide the enormous compost pile that receives
ongoing debris from my two-thirds-of-an-acre garden. This is a
long raised bed made of last season's compost, with the help of a
small tractor that shaped it into a berm. I'm using butterfly bushes for height: white ones that propagate so easily from tip cuttings, the dark purple 'Black Knight' and 'Purple Prince,' a brilliant
magenta cultivar. In front of these are shrub roses and blue and

pink flowering perennials billowing out over the front of the bed. On the bottom of the berm's back side I've planted several twelve-foot-tall giant Chinese silver grass (*Miscanthus floridulus*) for their screening value and silver tassels. Higher up on the berm, joe-pye weed (*Eupatorium purpureum*) with lavender umbrellalike flowers topping its eight-foot-tall stems should be just about high enough to join the grasses and butterfly bushes for a late summer symphony.

When I first saw *Rosa glauca* I couldn't believe it was a rose. This fascinating species of rose stands eight feet tall and equally wide, with arching canes that reach gracefully outward and downward. Spring leaves are burgundy, followed by single pink flowers in June that cover the branches. Plum-colored hips form that turn red-orange by fall and hold on during the winter. This intriguing shrub looks best at the back of a border and benefits from selective pruning to accentuate the arching shape of the canes. For use as a screening shrub, I would prune it less and let it thicken, as it tends to naturally.

In my own garden I've placed *Rosa glauca* toward the middle of a big freestanding mixed border so that it can be enjoyed from the house and from the road. I grow the dwarf lilac (*Syringa meyerii*) in front of it—its purple buds echo the rose's purplish-red leaf color. By the time *Rosa glauca*'s pink flowers appear, purple and magenta Siberian iris are flowering nearby, with dark pink-red peonies and blue Himalayan cranesbills (*Geranium himalayense*).

I saw the most exquisite use of *Rosa glauca* in Eleanor Fisher's English garden. Rosa glauca stood at the back of a border with the hybrid rugosa rose 'Roserie de L'Haye' in front of it and Siberian catmint (*Nepeta sibirica*) at the edge. The foliage and color contrasts were heavenly: fresh green crinkled leaves of the rugosa rose against the dark muted burgundy of *Rosa glauca*, the rich red-purple flower of the rugosa echoing the foliage of *Rosa glauca*, and blue-lavender spikes of Siberian catmint harmonizing with the purple and red-purple.

Rosa glauca can be grown in sun or shade. A striking composition in a shady Canadian border underplanted *Rosa glauca* with blue-green Siebold's hosta (*Hosta sieboldiana*) and lady's mantle (*Alchemilla mollis*) with its foam of small yellow-green flowers.

Several tall hybrid shrub roses also make effective informal hedges. The Grootendorst series of rugosa roses with red, pink, or white carnationlike flowers are tall enough to screen and thorny enough to discourage intruders. The nearly thornless English rose 'Heritage," has big double pastel pink roses all summer long, stands seven feet tall in its third year, and has shown no susceptibility to diseases or insect damage.

If you'd like an evergreen shrub with fall interest for screening, strawberry tree (*Arbutus unedo*) is handsome, especially in warmer climates. I grow a single plant on a sunny west corner where it thrives in shrubby form. A handsome planting in southern California consisted of an avenue of strawberry trees trained to single trunks. I've seen it used well as an informal hedge, too. The strawberry tree bears dark green, waxy small leaves, clusters of pendant white bell-shaped flowers and red-orange strawberry-like fruit that forms at the same time. Its bark is reddish-brown and has a shredded texture. Try autumn-flowering perennials at its base: blue plumbago (*Ceratostigma plumbaginoides*) would make a good carpet, along with California fuchsia flower (*Zauschneria californica*). Because my strawberry tree is near the door, I have underplanted it with Lenten (*Helleborus orientalis*) and Christmas rose (*Helleborus niger*) for winter blooms.

· SHRUBS FOR MID-BORDER ·

When I first began gardening, flowers were all I was interested in. As time passed and I visited many gardens, seeking to improve my own, I noticed that the best gardens mixed shrubs in along with the perennials—not just any old shrubs, but those with good form, long blooming period, and interesting leaves. They anchor a border, adding weight, volume, and solidity.

Shrubs for mid-border have to be the kind of plants that are horticulturally compatible with companions nearby. Hybrid tea roses, for example, need their own space, and flourish when planted in beds by themselves. Every time I've tried to mix them with perennials, they sulk and flower sparsely; their stiff canes always look out of place in a border. Many of the shrub roses, on the other hand, are more willing to share their growing space with other plants, and their rounded and spreading forms look more at home in the mixed border.

Hybrid musk roses are some of the best shrubs to combine with perennials. They usually grow four to five feet tall and spread five to seven feet across. Because they spread wider than they grow tall, they also make great trellis work for some of the smaller shrubby clematis, such as the six-foot-tall *Clematis recta*, with a foam of small white flowers, or *Clematis* × *durandii* with large blue-violet flowers. Hybrid musk roses flower all summer with clusters of single, semidouble and double flowers; nearly all are fragrant and will grow in partial shade. I have ordered every hybrid musk I could find for sale in the United States and Canada, and have never been disappointed. Forgive me if I rave, but these roses far surpass the popular hybrid teas, and should be sold in every nursery.

'Lavender Lassie' is actually rich deep pink with a hint of

lavender. This hybrid musk is very fragrant, and blooms continuously from July until frost, flourishing in partial shade. I love it with white astilbes, white-flowering *Clematis recta* and creamy-white *Artemisia lactiflora*, a tall, feathery-looking perennial that grows in the deeper shade behind 'Lavender Lassie.'

'Felicia' is a silvery-pink hybrid musk with extremely graceful double flowers that are beautiful as buds, too. I like to grow perennial *Salvia haematodes* nearby with its lavender-blue flower spikes that contrast well with the pastel pink roses. 'Rostock' is a very fragrant, pink hybrid musk. I like it surrounded by blue-violet balloon flowers (*Platycodon grandiflorus*) and purple *Salvia superba*.

'Mozart' is unique: single, flowers red on the edge, pink in the middle, with a white eye, bloom in profuse clusters, covering the shrub to create a reddish-pink effect. I can see it blazing away out in the garden from my office window, a good forty feet away, all summer long without a rest. White mallows bloom nearby, echoing the rose's white centers. 'Ballerina,' like 'Mozart,' is abundantly covered with trusses of single flowers, clear pink with white eyes; from a distance, they look pale pink.

'Cornelia' is delightful, with coppery coral buds opening to pink flowers. A sensational planting in New Zealand grouped 'Cornelia' with white foxgloves, white opium poppies, and blue forget-me-nots, bluer and taller than I'd ever seen, probably another plant entirely. The coral and pink tones of 'Cornelia' benefit from blue—try perennial 'Sunny Border Blue' veronica or annual 'Victoria' salvia.

I must mention two more hybrid musks. White semidouble 'Moonlight,' because I grow it in full shade with little water and it flowers profusely—it also has small, shiny dark-green leaves.

'Vanity' because of its unique pointed reddish-pink buds that open to large single hot-pink flowers with yellow centers that sit poised like butterflies at the tips of the branches.

English roses, the new hybrids introduced by David Austin, combine the fragrance and charm of the old roses with the re-bloom quality of the modern roses. They're marvelous in the mixed border. At the top of my list is 'Red Coat,' a single red rose-bush that flowers nonstop, summer and fall. I like it combined with cream scabious (*Scabiosa ochroleuca*), a perennial that looks like a pale yellow baby's breath. 'Hidcote' Saint-John's-wort (*Hypericum* 'Hidcote'), a shrubby perennial with bright yellow large single flowers, blooms nearly all summer nearby.

I hate to see the garden come to an abrupt halt when summer ends, so I put a lot of thought into shrubs for fall, those which flower, fruit, or turn glowing colors. Where I live, autumn is often our best season, with long days still warm enough to feel summery, yet without summer's blazing heat or spring's relentless rain.

Every fall I am struck by the full beauty of the late garden and how it easily rivals the earlier excitement of spring's flush. All the perennials and deciduous trees and shrubs are fully leafed out. There is the sweet fragrance of ripening fruit in the air and the awareness that there are still a couple of months of gardening left before winter closes down the show. It's like the last few hours of a good party, when the earlier trickle of strangers has melded together to become a group of friends, and the mood is one of easy, relaxed camaraderie. Plants have woven together in companionable groupings in the fullness of the autumn garden.

Fall is the season when the garden has settled down enough for me to sit on a bench and enjoy the garden. Any weeds left to pull are well hidden beneath foliage, and the slugs have departed

for wetter places. Besides, I'm too exhausted to care, and fall mel-
lowness is upon me. The light is soft, the sun more precious as the
days wane. Even the cats snuggle into warm corners as if to soak
up the last of the heat before winter arrives.

I came across my first bush clover (*Lespedeza thunbergii*) one fall
day in Francisca Dart's fascinating Canadian garden. When I ran
back to the house with great excitement and asked about the incredible shrub loaded with purplish-pink flowers and delicate
leaves, Francisca said in a casual voice, "Oh, that must be Lespedeza." Once again I swore not to get so worked up about a new
plant in front of a sophisticated gardener, but I'm quite hopeless
and continue my frenzied ways. Lespedeza went on my wish list,
and it took me a few years to find it in a mail-order catalog. When
it grew up and flowered, it turned out to be white, and is probably
Lespedeza japonica or *Lespedeza thunbergii* 'Albiflora.' I don't much care
what it's called—it's gorgeous, flowers in early fall with small
white blooms cascading at the tops of the six-foot arching stems.
Dwarf asters in shades of blue and lavender and lavender Russian
sage (*Perovskia atriplicifolia*) are fine companions.

Another Latin tongue-twister, *Leycesteria formosa*, commonly
called Himalayan honeysuckle, is a subtle, novel beauty for the fall
garden. This medium-sized shrub has thick green hollow stems
that look a little like bamboo in winter. Spring leaves are pointed
and flushed with tints of reddish-brown. Chains of white flowers
surrounded by dark burgundy bracts dangle from branch ends in
fall, finally forming dark, shiny black berries. I grow it close to the
edge of a small, south-facing bed where I can see its unusual bracts
easily; from a distance they're too dark to be noticed.

I've so often admired beautyberry (*Callicarpa bodinieri*) in fall
gardens that my friends took the hint and gave me one for Christ-

mas. Iridescent lilac-purple fruits that look even showier after the leaves drop are beautyberry's main attraction, and the shrub stands out best against a needle evergreen. Several are better than one, if you have the room, with carpets of fall-flowering cyclamen (*Cyclamen hederifolium*) nearby.

A group of red chokeberries (*Aronia arbutifolia*) caught my eye one fall day; their leaves were blazing red, their branches were loaded with red berries. The variety 'Brilliantissima' is known for especially bright berry color. Compact cranberry bush (*Viburnum opulus* 'Compactum') stole the show in a small fall garden with handsome, brilliant red oaklike leaves and clusters of bright red fruits. And oakleaf hydrangea (*Hydrangea quercifolia*) turns heads in the fall when its oak-shaped leaves color up burgundy.

· FRONTLINE SHRUBS ·

It's always a challenge to find well-behaved low-growing shrubs for the front of a border, beneath low windows, and near the front entry. In my first garden, the walkway to the front door was flanked by hybrid tea roses. Although the fragrance and color was marvelous all summer long, I'm sure the mail carrier could have done without the thorns. And, much as I love roses, their canes in winter are not appealing; they work best where they won't be noticed when they're dormant.

The ideal small shrub that all my clients want is evergreen, flowers for a long time in shade or sun, is fragrant, makes a low mound, doesn't need pruning, has no diseases, and can be found in the local nursery. I try to keep a straight face while agreeing that yes, it would be nice if there were a plant this perfect, but since there isn't, why don't we blend a number of plants that combined have all these good traits and form a tapestry.

Several low evergreen shrubs offer good leaves and form without much in the way of flowers. 'Helleri' Japanese dwarf holly is a handsome low-mounding plant with dark green leaves. Privet honeysuckle (*Lonicera pileata*) has low horizontal branches covered with small shiny dark green leaves. Box honeysuckle (*Lonicera nitida*) grows a bit taller with tiny dark green glossy leaves. A yellow-leaved selection of box honeysuckle, 'Baggesen's Gold' introduces bright leaves instead of flowers. Evergreen huckleberry (*Vaccinium ovatum*) contributes reddish-brown new foliage and edible fruit.

Variegated leaves add valuable color, lighting up dark corners. I am very fond of variegated box, especially the creamy-yellow kind (*Buxus sempervirens* 'Aureovariegata'). These can be grown informally or clipped into tidy shapes or hedges. In a remarkable formal garden in Christschurch, New Zealand, these variegated boxes were clipped into cones and stood like sentries at the corners of the flower beds. Occasionally they were placed on opposite sides of a path, as guardian shrubs, as if to say "enter here." To echo their variegated leaves, a ground cover of variegated rock cress (*Arabis ferdinandi-coburgii* 'Variegata') drifted nearby. In my own garden I cut branches of this variegated box in winter with early 'February Gold' daffodils; the box lasts for weeks in the vase and looks pretty alone when the daffodils fade.

Several varieties of *Euonymus fortunei radicans* have lovely variegated foliage; these low-growing shrubs can spread, drape, or weave. 'Emerald Gaiety' is my favorite, with green and creamy-white leaves; 'Emerald and Gold' is green and bright yellow, while 'Silver Queen' starts out green and yellow in spring and turns green and creamy-white by summer. In deep shade, try *Vinca major* 'Elegantissima' with dark green glossy leaves and creamy-yellow variegation.

Gray leaves please me a great deal. Senecio 'Sunshine' with lightly furred oval leaves makes a fine low shrub in full sun. The woolly willow (*Salix lanata*) is on my wish list—its silvery leaves catch your eye from a great distance. Gray santolina serves well as a low, spreading gray mound, and can also be clipped into a low hedge. Blue-green rue makes a low shrub or a hedge; its unusual color complements pink and red flowers.

Small shrubs for the front of the border can be used to support floppy perennials and shrubby clematis. At Powys Castle in Wales, a low boxwood hedge kept the spiderwort (*Tradescantia virginiana*) behind it from falling on its face and gave the peonies a frame to lean against.

I'm just beginning to experiment with combining shrubs and vines, after reading these words of encouragement by Christopher Lloyd:

> *Every mature shrub of reasonable proportions should be regarded from time to time with a questioning: "How would you look with a clematis growing over you?"*

Rosemary Verey shows some inspiring examples of shrubs threaded with clematis in *The Art of Planting*. Surely we cannot go wrong by following in the footsteps of such masterful gardeners.

In my own garden I'm weaving the indigo-blue shrubby *Clematis durandii* through a dwarf gray-leaved willow. I've seen photographs of the same blue clematis draping over Senecio 'Sunshine,' a gray-leaved shrub with yellow flowers.

And now for the smaller deciduous shrubs that contribute seasonal color through leaves and flowers. Daphne 'Carol Mackie' with lavender-pink fragrant spring flowers and green leaves edged with creamy white is at the top of my list. So are tree peonies (*Paeonia suffruticosa*), woody shrubs with beautifully indented leaves and enormous showy flowers in spring. Blooms have feathery edges, giving the plant a breathtaking delicacy—colors are pink, lavender, dark lacquered red, white, and yellow.

Blue mist (*Caryopteris clandonensis*) is a low-key beauty that flowers in late summer at about the same time that the fall-flowering sedums (*Sedum spectabile*) are beginning to show some color. Caryopteris stays blue into the fall when its color pairs up well with the coral kaffir lily (*Schizostylis coccinea*).

The shrubby cinquefoil (*Potentilla fruticosa*) is a carefree summer bloomer; it usually has yellow flowers. 'Abbotswood' is a choice cultivar for the front of the border with gray-green leaves and white flowers. If you feel daring, try maroon 'Crimson Pygmy' barberry (*Berberis thunbergii* 'Crimson Pygmy') for a strong color accent. Cool it off with blue or lavender flowers nearby, heat it up with yellow or red accompaniment, or set it off with silver foliage.

Although it doesn't flower, the dwarf cranberry bush (*Viburnum opulus* 'Nanum') is a good-looking small deciduous shrub with red winter twigs and attractive oaklike leaves that turn red in the fall. Use it for a winter accent in Japanese style gardens; place it close to the path to better appreciate the red twigs. I've also seen it used as a low hedge in front of a porch, and as an underplanting to surround a piece of sculpture poised on a stump.

Eight

. . . .

Garden

. . . .

Structures

I built my first garden structure because the old grapevines that were dotted around the property needed support. I found them lying on the ground and leaning against an assortment of rusty metal fence posts and rotting wooden stakes. The flower gardener in me had a long argument with the conservationist.

"Rip them out and make a flower border!"

"No, save those old vines with the interesting gnarled trunks and train them up and over an arbor."

"What do I need all those grapes for?"

"It would be too great a waste to tear them all out. Besides, you have two-thirds of an acre and plenty of space for flower borders."

In the end, I didn't have the heart to pull out the tough old grapes. Even though everyone else thought I should train them horizontally on posts and wires, the way all the books tell you to, I didn't want my garden looking like a vineyard. In my mind's eye, I saw a grape arbor with tall posts supporting an overhead gridded canopy. I imagined training the old vines up and over this ceiling and pictured heavy purple clusters of juicy grapes hanging through the grid. This way I could save the grapes and also enjoy the way they looked.

Arbors give a garden architectural structure and shade while supporting vining plants that provide fragrance, color, and fruit. In hot climates a shady walkway is especially inviting. A garden I once visited in California had an extensive pergola built along the far perimeter of the garden. Walking beneath it I stayed cool in summer's heat and enjoyed catching glimpses of the main garden beds and borders. Grapes and clematis fruiting and flowering overhead added to my delight while I strolled beneath the pergola. I had a second chance to admire this beautiful structure when I saw it from inside the house. Most good garden structures serve this kind of double duty: beautiful within the garden and lovely for viewing from a distance. Place them where they will offer this maximal enjoyment, in plain view from the windows, or from the patio.

Pergolas are walkways, so they help lead you from one garden room to another, like a hall inside the house. A heavenly per-

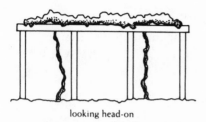

looking head-on

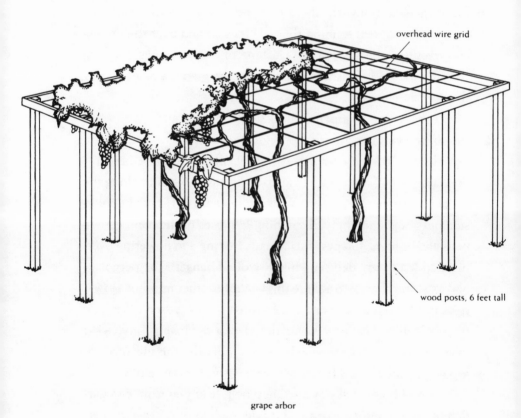

overhead wire grid

wood posts, 6 feet tall

grape arbor

gola in New Zealand, covered with white climbing 'Iceberg' roses, invited you to walk from the main open lawn of the front garden to a rose garden edged with lavender. An old-fashioned garden in Seattle had a pergola covered with wisteria; the long, fragrant chains of lavender flowers dangled through an overhead grid. This structure served as a corridor, leading you on a stroll from one part of the garden to another. A pergola can also function as a shady canopy to sit beneath, perhaps attached to a deck or patio.

I love garden arches with built-in benches at the base. That way you can sit in the shade, enjoying the vining flowers over-head, and look out to the garden panorama. The benches are also handy for standing on when training and pruning your overhead vines. By standing on the benches below my garden arch, I can just about reach high enough to tie, train, and groom the pink 'New Dawn' rose overhead. Two long sticks help me maneuver the canes where the arch is just beyond my reach. With hindsight, I'd plant a thornless climber instead of 'New Dawn'—'Zephirine Drouhin,' a Bourbon rose with deep pink, fragrant flowers, or David Austin's pastel-pink 'Heritage.' Both of these are technically shrub roses, but each is tall enough to be encouraged to climb. Their thornless canes make them much safer near benches.

Two outstanding gardeners in Estacada, Oregon have a se-ries of arches with built-in benches along the perimeter of their garden, facing in toward the main perennial beds. These are well-used resting places to stop, sit, and admire the flowers. A glider stationed along the way invites you to relax. Whimsical, hand-made wooden birdhouses and feeders are mounted on posts in front of protective shrubs. Under an old apple tree, rustic wood-en chairs and tables welcome the visitor. All of these useful orna-ments embellish the garden's beauty.

Benches that are built into existing decks, porches, or arches are so much easier on the gardener than freestanding furniture—you don't have to move them every time you mow the lawn. Wide benches built to surround a large tree trunk are especially useful. Make them wide enough to sit and visit with friends, rest your glasses of iced tea, and stash a few garden books, too.

Garden sheds can be useful and beautiful if they are constructed with both intentions kept in mind. Used to store tools and garden supplies, with a potting bench and storage bins, they can look like small guesthouses from the outside if windows and window boxes planted with colorful annuals are included. Train a rose up one wall and let it scramble over the roofline. Make a path of stepping-stones to the door, and plant Corsican mint in the crevices. Every time you walk to the shed you will enjoy the fresh minty fragrance. If you routinely take a wheelbarrow or mowing equipment to the shed, it might be more practical to pave a smooth path to the entry, and line it on both sides with lavender hedges or cottage pinks for fragrance. Paint a mural on one wall for an artful touch, or hang a ceramic garden hat.

If you are a serious propagator, a greenhouse built to look charming can become a focal point in your garden. Wood-and-glass or metal-and-glass greenhouses look best to me, and there are many attractive styles to choose from. Low plantings at the base of the greenhouse, or a small vine trained along one wall can help join it to the garden.

Although a greenhouse is still on my wish list, I am fortunate to have a potting shed, built by a generous friend who could see how much I needed to screen the messy-looking pots, potting soil and flats. It's actually a roofless enclosure with walls made of wooden fencing material, capped by a decorative lattice trim, designed to match my neighbor's fence. I've trained an akebia vine up through the lattice and hopefully into the plum tree overhead. (Any structure in my garden is an excuse for a vine.)

Old fruit trees can become trellises for big climbing roses; rambling roses that scramble up the tree, with their flower sprays draping down over the branches in a graceful fashion are best. The mauve rambler 'Veilchenblau,' covering an old fruit tree with garlands of flowers in a New Zealand garden, is etched in my memory. The white 'Seagull' rose blooms forever on a slide I took in an English garden, where it shone way at the top of a big old fruit tree. To successfully grow a climber up a tree, make a huge hole out toward the drip line, fill it with aged compost, add some slow-release fertilizer, plant the rose, and water well. Train the rose toward the lower branches with twine or a stake. Keep watering well until it is established, and give it a helping hand up the tree for the first season or two until it gains a foothold.

Old trees can also be turned into displays of birdhouses and feeders. Stumps can be covered with honeysuckle or clematis. A slender tree stump can serve as a pedestal for a water basin, or a piece of sculpture; a fat one can be planed down to become a simple stool. Imagination is a gift that can turn raw materials into beauty. My favorite garden bench, made by Brian A. Symes, is built of fallen cedar. He used a curved limb for the top rail of the backrest, and I love to look at that gracefully bowed line from my office window. It's as beautiful as a piece of sculpture.

Fences and walls are garden structures just waiting to be embellished by vines. I staple plastic netting to wooden fences and twine honeysuckle and clematis through the grid. Often the vines will continue to travel, hurling themselves up the neighbor's plum and laurel. Even unattractive cyclone fencing can become a tapestry of flowers if you plant clematis vines at the base and weave them through the metal mesh. A solid wooden fence can become home for espaliered sasanqua camellias; thread some screw eyes into the fence and tie your vine at intervals to the screw eyes.

· FINDING YOUR GARDEN ORNAMENTS ·

Craftsmen and gardeners are kindred spirits, striving to fashion beauty for daily enjoyment. Since I am self-employed, I like to support fellow artists and craftsmen working on their own, and urge you to do the same. Craft fairs, markets, and garden shows are becoming increasingly popular where I live, and they are fine places to meet local artists. Art galleries often showcase outdoor garden art, and well-run nurseries and lumberyards can often refer you to a skilled craftsman. Word of mouth is another good way to find a carpenter, sculptor, or potter who can custom-make the garden structure or ornament that you are dreaming of.

I found my garden furniture by inquiring at a friend's garden—where had she found her comfortable cedar chairs and tables? I had been sitting in them for an hour, so I knew the chairs were more than pretty to look at. My friend sent me to see George Ledbury, a retired millworker, out in the country, who simply couldn't stop working. His prices were so reasonable that I would have bought more than I needed if it weren't for the limits of my small station wagon. As it was, we spent half an hour trying to figure out how to cram four chairs and two end tables into the car!

Cedar, redwood and teak are long-lasting woods that weather well outdoors. Cast iron and wrought iron are sturdy and attractive too, but heavier to move around. Because I respect my back, I prefer to stick to wooden furniture, but I frequently admire wrought-iron gates, railings, and trelliswork. Look under "iron" in the Yellow Pages for craftsmen, or ask in a garden featuring iron ornaments.

Sometimes you can luck out at estate sales, garage sales, and even businesses that are closing down. A friend bought a beautiful teak screen from a restaurant that was going out of business—it makes a super focal point in his garden. I have heard stories of sensational finds at the local dump, thrift shops, and rummage sales.

If you hire an artisan to custom-make a bench, arch or garden gate, draw a sketch of what your vision looks like, or find a photograph that comes close. Otherwise you run the risk of losing too much in the translation between words and the finished product. Your best bet is to see the artisan's sample pieces or at least to browse through his or her portfolio.

If you prefer to shop by mail, Barbara Barton's excellent source book, *Gardening by Mail* lists many vendors of garden furniture and ornaments in the section titled "Garden Suppliers and Services." Her detailed descriptions tell you all about the styles offered, materials used, and catalog costs. Be aware that the cost of brokering, shipping, handling, and advertising may add significantly to your final price.

· SCULPTURE IN THE GARDEN ·

I often reflect on how lucky I have been to meet so many gifted gardeners, artists, and writers who have come to see my garden or have shown up in a garden class. Sometimes, tied to my garden, I miss the adventure of traveling more, but then I realize how my garden itself has been a magnet, attracting marvelous visitors my way—another form of adventure.

A fortunate introduction brought a remarkable sculptor, Katy Mcfadden-Benecki, to my garden in 1989. Katy makes high-fired outdoor terra-cotta garden sculpture, and we thought my garden might be a good place to display her pieces. With some trepidation, I watched Katy unload life-size and larger-than-life-size human figures from her truck onto a hand truck and wheel them into the garden. We took some time placing them where they would look most at home in the garden, surrounded by flowering plants.

Before long I began to enjoy these creatures so much that I secretly hoped they wouldn't sell. The terra-cotta color and solidity complement the soft textures and colors of the plants, while adding the company of human and animal forms. Two larger-than-life-size sunbathing women lean against each other at the front of a bed filled with colorful perennials. Their presence turns the bed into a meadow. A sleeping gardener rests peacefully on his side beneath a small plum tree. My cats often join him for a nap—once I did, too! Garden hats made of glazed ceramic fool the eye until touched—they hang from hidden nails on the tree trunks.

Iridescent raku fish are made with holes in their bellies, designed to receive iron rods stuck in the ground. They perch permanently on the rods and look as if they're swimming through the ferny foliage of love-in-a-mist (*Nigella*). Some make their way through the red reedy foliage of Japanese bloodgrass (*Imperata cylindrica 'Rubra'*). The rods disappear in the foliage: the fish hover above.

Garden ornaments of stone, marble, bronze, or cast iron can give your garden an added touch of whimsy or eternity depending on the theme. Pan or Saint Francis will each set a special mood. Sculpture personalizes the garden, telling the world a little more about the gardener's taste, values, and sense of humor. Even concrete garden frogs can look serious or silly, depending on the expression on their faces.

· WATER IN THE GARDEN ·

Cynthia Spencer introduced water to my garden when she brought her terra-cotta birdbaths and water basins. I love these as focal points toward the front of the flower beds. The water brings birds, and adds its cool, serene reflective surface to the garden on hot summer days.

I don't have a pond yet, but someday I'd like to. Still water is tranquil, reflective, and soothing. It can be a home for water plants, birds, fish, frogs, and insects. Children will head straight for water to check out the wildlife. Because its surface reflects light by day and by moonlight, water makes the garden look larger, mirroring the color of flowers and sky. At Van Dusen Gardens in Vancouver, British Columbia pink astilbes and yellow candelabra primroses (*Primula florindae*) blooming at the lake's edge are doubled in number by reflection. Water lilies and ducks adorn the water's surface. A path designed for strolling surrounds the lake, allowing you to meander and enjoy views across the water.

Ponds and pools can be designed on a small scale for your home garden. Be sure to place them where you will most enjoy seeing them. Too often I've seen ponds at the farthest end of the garden, added on almost as an afterthought. One sensational water feature that made better sense was at the entry to a home where a series of fountains were installed for enjoyment on a daily basis, coming and going, and in view of the windows. A small pool, or even an old stone trough filled with water, can bring a small amount of reflective surface to the entry garden.

Water features can reduce the amount of mowing, and even solve the problem of what to do with ground that is too uneven, dry, wet, or difficult to plant. When one of my friends saw how soggy my soil was in the winter, she suggested that I turn the backyard into a lake. At the time I was horrified, but years later I can see that she had a good idea!

Because of the play of light on the surface of water, you're better off placing water features in sun. Stay away from trees—the leaf litter will dirty the water.

Moving water brings new dimensions to your garden. The power of a waterfall and its hypnotic effect can cleanse the mind after a busy day out in the world. Rivers and creeks add movement, sound, and glinting light. Site your house and garden to take maximal advantage of these natural features if you're lucky enough to have them on your property. Watching a river for a few minutes slows down the inner world, rests the overworked brain, soothes the eyes.

To create a water feature that looks natural, study nature and observe the shapes, angles, and curves that form our rivers, streams, and ponds. The best book I know for ideas is *The Water Garden* by Anthony Paul and Yvonne Rees. It is chock full of specific how-to information with marvelous photographs and illustrations. You can get ideas from water-garden suppliers, such as Lilypons Water Gardens and Van Ness Water Gardens. *Gardening by Mail* lists more than a dozen water-garden vendors.

Because I've seen so many cracked ponds and man-made creeks that look more like ditches, I urge you to screen carefully before hiring a contractor to build a water feature. Where I live, there are only a handful of top-notch water-garden designers. I've seen their work in gardens and wouldn't settle for less. This is a major structural addition to the garden and deserves the same se-lective screening process as finding a good builder. Ask for refer-ences; look at portfolio photographs; visit several gardens to see the designer's work before you invest. And be prepared to wait in line—a good water-garden designer will have a full schedule.

Nine

Garden Design Challenges

Perfect gardens exist only in paradise and in our dreams. Real life gives us irregular ground, unpredictable weather, and miserable soil. These obstacles test our mettle. If we begin to see these difficulties as opportunities to stretch our imaginations, we can accomplish miracles. Nearly every garden has at least one challenging aspect that gives us the chance to rise to the occasion.

· DRY SHADE ·

The toughest place to garden is at the base of large, dense-canopied trees with strong surface-root systems that drain every ounce of water and nutrition from the soil. In my garden a deodar cedar, hawthorn, and the neighbor's apple trees have staked their claim to one area and refuse to share their space with anything but ivy. Because they provide habitat for birds and squirrels and screen my garden, I have left them alone. If you are facing a similar dilemma, ask yourself whether the trees have enough value to compensate for the difficulty or impossibility of gardening at their base. Do they offer canopy, screening, windbreak, winter interest? Do they shelter wildlife? If not—and they're simply occupying valuable space—consider taking them out. You get no extra credit for suffering with unattractive, useless plants. Remove the trees and have the stumps ground out to ease future planting. You have now liberated a new area for gardening.

If the existing trees do offer beauty or utility, you can take some steps to improve gardening beneath them. First, see whether you can prune selectively to open the trees, admitting more light and rainfall to the ground below. Then see whether you can improve the existing soil to create some planting pockets. Don't try this near magnolias—they resent having their roots pestered—but most trees will accept some soil improvement between the hard fingers of their surface roots. Be careful not to alter the soil line around the trunk, and for best results cultivate and plant toward the drip line. Explore slowly, looking for places to dig your shovel into, and add compost to the existing soil to make a friendlier, more nourishing and water-retentive medium for new plants. Remember that trees will continue to take the lion's share of water, so baby your new plants for at least the first year with water, fertilizer, and mulch. Mulch will keep the soil moist and help smother weeds.

A variety of ingredients will help improve soil in dry shade, including manure, compost, gypsum and peat moss.

No pudding could be more complicated than the preparation of

a garden soil; as far as I have been able to find out, dung,

manure, guano, leafmold, sods, humus, sand, straw, lime,

kainit, Thomas's powder, baby powder, saltpeter, horn,

phosphates, droppings, cow dung, ashes, peat, compost, water,

beer, knocked-out pipes . . . and many other substances

are added. After his death the gardener does not become a

butterfly . . . but a garden worm tasting all the dark

nitrogenous, and spicy delights of the soil.

—Karel Capek

The Gardener's Year

All gardeners who have seen the improvement in plant growth and health that results from soil improvement get very excited about compost, and eventually learn to make their own the better to enjoy the sight of shiny red earthworms wriggling around at the bottom of the pile. Gardeners like to talk about making compost the way cooks like to discuss recipes, and would rather get compost for Christmas than jewelry.

You can make your own compost in a tidy arrangement of bins, with a system of forking the material from one bin to the next as it decomposes, or you can simply make piles and wait for them to rot. The second way works as well as the first, but takes longer. I simply pile grass clippings, annual weeds, leaves, soft vegetable kitchen waste, and used-up potting soil to a height of four feet or more and wait. I have plenty of other work to do meanwhile, so it doesn't seem to take that long.

When I am seriously building better soil in my garden, I invite all my neighbors and friends to bring me bagged leaves and grass clippings. Landscaping friends deliver and dump pickup loads of mown grass onto tarps which I then drag to the future beds, piling all the garden debris into tall heaps. Neighbors with rabbits and chickens are happy to have you clean out the droppings unless they are clever enough to be composting themselves.

Adding soil to the pile speeds the breakdown process, but I find there is enough soil from weeds and old potting soil to do the job. A four-foot pile will collapse into a one-foot raised bed after a winter of rain. I usually gather these piles exactly where I plan to make a new bed the following spring, and plant directly in the newly formed compost. Some prefer to rototill or hand-spade the compost into the existing soil to mix it all up. It works either way—the critical part is to water your new plants faithfully during their first year or two to help them establish strong root systems. In following years you can be less vigilant, if you choose drought-tolerant shade lovers.

Begin by selecting a few sturdy shrubs for the understory, which connects the tall canopy of trees to the ground-covering lower plants. Tough shrubs are the tried-and-true survivors that might be considered invasive or common in better soil. Portuguese laurel (*Prunus lusitanica*) is highly recommended by Beth Chatto. This is a handsome, tall evergreen shrub noted for its dark, glossy leaves, showy spikes of creamy-white flowers, and clusters of red to dark purple fall berries. In dense shade this aggressive plant earns its keep.

Oregon grape (*Mahonia aquifolium*) has spiny-toothed leaves and showy clusters of yellow spring flowers, followed by dark blue berries that make a good jelly. Common as bread and scorned for its suckering habit, it is a gift in the dry shade garden. I am fond of the shorter species, longleaf mahonia (*Mahonia nervosa*), a two-foot tall spreading ground cover that looks right at home in a woodland garden, where the rhythm of its pinnate leaflets leaning obliquely makes a lovely pattern.

Heavenly bamboo (*Nandina domestica*) is an excellent evergreen shrub that has bamboo's willowy appearance without its invasive nature. Slim, tapered leaves, panicles of white flowers, red berries and bronzy-red fall color distinguish this six-foot-tall plant. Its upright form and loose habit shows us the breeze moving through it. Flower arrangers appreciate its fall berries and interesting foliage.

The buttercuplike single yellow spring flowers of *Kerria japonica* offer a cheering note in the dark shade garden. Slender bright-green branches that light up the winter garden leaf out in spring with pointed, toothed, handsomely veined leaves that turn yellow in fall. With room enough to spread its arching branches, kerria makes a lovely focal point in shade, like many garlands of single yellow roses. Its double form, 'Pleniflora,' is less graceful as a plant, suckering and spreading into a thick tangle of branches. However, I once had the pleasure of seeing its curved, cut branches covered with small, charming double yellow flowers laid out down the center of a long dinner table. With a plant that's so abundant, though untidy, it's easier to cut flowers for the table in good conscience.

In my own garden, Japanese aralia (*Fatsia japonica*), an unlikely-looking shrub, thrives in dry shade. I did give it plenty of water the first spring I moved it in and during the summer of that same year. Three years later, it flourishes with little attention. This is a shrub that you love or hate, as its large, glossy, hand-shaped leaves give it a tropical, imposing character. I love it for sentimental and aesthetic reasons. I saw my first plant outside the dentist's window and its broad leaves gave me a calming strength at every visit. Grateful that he planted this for consolation and aware that it got no special care, I planted one on the drab north side of my first house where its height and shine were welcome. In extreme cold its leaves blackened, but it always leafed out with renewed vigor after spring pruning. My current aralia lives in the inhospitable shade of an old, majestic deodar cedar, where its glossy green leaves illuminate the dark. In the same place where rhododendrons and hydrangeas bit the dust, aralia flourishes. The good health of an ordinary plant is worth ten times the value of a languishing exotic one.

Ressembling the aralia, x *Fatshedera lizei* is a sprawling evergreen that can spread overground or be trained as a vine. A lovely memory of it trained on a stone wall in an old neglected garden reminds me of its virtue in dry shade. Planted some distance away from the aralia, it could mimic the same leaf shape yet offer a different growing habit, covering an old stump or decorating a fence.

There is an abundance of ground covers for dry shade. Two of my favorites, the evergreen winter-flowering bear's-foot hellebore (*Helleborus foetidus*) and spring-flowering Mrs. Robb's spurge

(*Euphorbia robbiae*) have already been described in Chapter 5. These two look handsome beside each other, and they spread at fairly similar rates. I like to group them beneath trees or at the edge of a path to frame the bed. The evergreen bishop's hat (*Epimedium*) is another excellent ground cover with heart-shaped leaves; this one establishes more slowly. Choose its strongest growing cultivar, *Epimedium* × *versicolor* 'Sulphureum,' with yellow flowers, for dry shade. Amazingly showy in winter, evergreen Lenten rose (*Helleborus orientalis*) will also establish itself in dry shade if the soil is improved before planting and the plant is watered regularly during its first year.

Thriving on neglect, the bright-green leaves of sweet woodruff (*Galium odoratum*) that grow in whorled fashion around the stems expand quickly into sheets of fresh green ground cover, bursting into delicate, fragrant white sprays of flowers in May. Interplant some lily-of-the-valley (*Convallaria majalis*), so invasive that any gardener will be happy to foist some extras on you, and you will have additional fragrance from its sweet stems of white bells. One small bouquet of lily-of-the-valley will perfume a room. These petite flowers have big leaves that turn yellow in summer; they can be trimmed off with no regrets when interplanted with another ground cover like sweet woodruff.

Hardy geranium, commonly called cranesbill to describe its seedpod, is adaptable nearly everywhere, and the most aggressive kinds can tough it out in dry shade. Pick the plants that are pests anywhere else and plant them where their persistence will be a virtue. Foot-tall *Geranium macrorrhizum* with rounded leaves and magenta flowers carpets the ground at the base of trees where little else will survive. Finding its way everywhere in my garden by runner and seed, *Geranium* × *oxonianum* 'Claridge Druce' is a mixed blessing. Flowering bright pink nearly all summer, it is welcome in dry shade, but I do have to shovel out heaps of it where it gallops across the astilbes and threatens to climb the hydrangeas. Charming as it looks at the base of awkward, leggy shrub roses, its exuberance knows no limits, and you must treat it with a firm hand.

Similarly rampant, lady's mantle (*Alchemilla mollis*) and purple Labrador violet (*Viola labrodorica purpurpea*) are great ground covers for dry shade, with attractive leaves and long bloom periods. Lady's mantle sports lobed leaves and sprays of yellow-green flowers, while the violet has purplish leaves and violet flowers. They can serve as edgers along a path or in carpeting drifts beneath trees and shrubs, traveling by root and seed.

Less aggressive, hardy cyclamen provides lovely ground-covering heart-shaped leaves that are green or green marbled with silver. Buy them leafed out in their pots for the best selection of foliage patterns. Fall-flowering *Cyclamen hederifolium* and winter-flowering *Cyclamen coum* bring pink or white flowers to the garden at unexpected times of the year. Very much like shooting stars (*Dodecatheon meadia*), cyclamen flowers have extremely reflexed petals and look like they're poised for flight. I love to see groups of bright-pink *Cyclamen coum* flowering on a February afternoon as much as I like to see pink or white *Cyclamen hederifolium* shooting up above the fallen leaves in autumn.

For some height in dry shade, goat's beard (*Aruncus dioicus*) with its ferny leaves and plumy cream-colored flowers makes a strong solitary statement as it stretches six or seven feet tall and three to four feet across. Architectural, it stands best alone, rising above ground cover, with hosta or lady's mantle at its feet. Three-foot-tall Solomon's seal (*Polygonatum* × *hybridum*) is described eloquently by Graham Stuart Thomas in "Perennial Garden Plants":

The stems bear along their arching length broad, horizon-
tally poised leaves and little bells of greeny white in
clusters. . . . The ideal companion is a lacy fern.

I find the repeated rhythm of all these vertical bells juxtaposed
against the pattern of horizontal lines of the leaves enchanting.
My Solomon's seal grows in front of the larger-leaved Japanese aralia (*Fatsia japonica*) with the dissected leaves of autumm fern (*Dry-*
opteris erythrosora) nearby.

Cream and white flowers help illuminate shady places. So do
leaves variegated with cream, pale yellow, or white. The dark
green waxy leaves of *Vinca major* 'Elegantissima' always catch my
eye in shade garden because of their creamy yellow marking. So
do the dissected leaves of variegated goutweed (*Aegopodium*
podograria 'Variegata'). The word "weed" should set off flashing red
lights and sound bells warning you against growing plants so
named, at least anywhere but dry shade, where you seek the
cream of the weed crop.

Western sword fern (*Polystichum munitum*) and autumn fern
(*Dryopteris erythrosora*) have done well for me in dry shade, adding
an elegance of form and evergreen foliage, rising three feet tall to
hover gracefully above lower ground covers. Judith Jones, emi-
nent Northwest fern grower, describes the autumn fern lyrically
in her "Fancy Fronds" catalog:

Exotic coppery-pink croziers unroll into pinkish honey-
green fleshy fronds which mature to a rich leathery green.
Cold weather brings a hint of russet to this peerless ever-
green. As if all this display were not enough, it produces
bright red sori on the frond reverse in late summer.

· MOIST SHADE ·

Shade cast by the house, a wall or fence is a much friendlier environment for plants, as the ground there will be cool and moist.
Improving the soil with compost and well-rotted manure is still
recommended, to improve fertility and drainage. Once the ground
is prepared, new plants will spread their roots more freely than in
dry shade, as long as you remember to choose shade lovers.

Where height is needed, small trees or large shrubs can be
planted. Winter-flowering witch hazel (*Hamamelis*) is an outstanding specimen, growing twelve to fifteen feet tall and spreading as
wide or wider, with fragrant, ribbonlike petals flowering on bare
branches in shades of yellow, coppery-orange, or reddish-orange.
Its bold leaves remind me of filbert, and they turn yellow in the
fall. In "Ornamental Shrubs, Climbers, and Bamboos," Graham
Stuart Thomas recommends *Hamamelis mollis* 'Pallida':

> It is a pearl beyond price, with its very bright light yellow,
> sweetly scented flowers of good quality, and lightens the
> garden on the dullest day. A magnificent contrast to the
> purple-copper leaves of Rhododendron ponticum *var.*
> purpureum.

Witch hazel benefits from a small-leaved evergreen backdrop to
set off its winter flowers.

Smoke tree (*Cotinus coggygria*) grows well in moist shade; its
rounded leaves remind me of eucalyptus. I enjoy both the blue-
green leaves of smoke tree and the rich, dramatic foliage of its
'Royal Purple' cultivar. I prune off branches of this small tree and
use them in flower arrangements.

Stewartia pseudocamellia prefers to be in shade and makes an elegant specimen, with late summer flowers like single white camellias. It has red-and-yellow fall leaf color and winter bark like an abstract painting of tan, cream, and gray patches, so smooth that you must run your hand down the trunk. Japanese snowbell (*Styrax japonica*) will flourish in shade and adorns the early summer garden with its delicate white bells.

There are many shrubs for moist shade. *Disanthus cercidifolius*, a tall, deciduous shrub with heart-shaped leaves, is at its best in autumn when the foliage turns red, orange and mahogany. In spring its leaves are fresh green in contrast to burgundy stems. A planting in an artist's garden placed dwarf purple barberry in front of the disanthus to echo the stem color. For a low-key planting, try a carpet of sweet woodruff beneath it, or repeat the heart-shaped leaves by underplanting with bishop's hat (Epimedium) which will stay evergreen in winter.

Hydrangeas are invaluable in the shade garden and are happiest growing in moist, fertile soil. There are many species and cultivars, all with substantial flowers, blooming in summer and lasting into fall. The oakleaf hydrangea (*Hydrangea quercifolia*) is prized for its shapely oaklike leaves that turn crimson in fall. Although this hydrangea flourishes in shade, its leaves color up best in full sun. Its ivory flowers are oblong, like butterfly bush, and grow sideways rather than straight up. The oval, glossy leaves and red fall berries of evergreen wintergreen (*Gaultheria procumbens*) make a subtle underplanting to complement the bold oakleaf hydrangea. A clump or two of bronzeleaf rodgersia (*Rodgersia podophylla*) nearby would echo the hydrangea's leaves and repeat the creamy colored flowers in a more plumy form.

Bigleaf hydrangea (*Hydrangea macrophylla*) comes round-headed and lace-capped. An acid soil will turn the flowers bluer; an alkaline or limy soil will encourage pinker flowers. There are named cultivars with reliably pink, white, or blue flowers. You can cut hydrangea flowers for drying and wreath making or leave them alone to enjoy them in the fall garden. I love hydrangeas massed, with tons of astilbes nearby, making an ocean of pink, blue, and cream colors in damp shade. My favorite hydrangea, so far, is *Hydrangea serrata* 'Preziosa,' with dark wine-colored stems, and rose-pink flowers that darken to a mixture of burgundy, cherry-red and plum colors. Their colors remind me of a pointillist painting or a tapestry footstool, old-fashioned and charming with a blended muted richness. *Hydrangea villosa* is on my wish list. I saw it in a Canadian garden and could hardly tear myself away from its tapered velvety leaves and huge purplish-pink lacecap flowers.

The hardy fuchsia (*Fuchsia magellanica*) has a delicate grace that can subtly adorn the shade garden. Small-leaved, with an abundance of narrow, pendant, bell-shaped flowers, bicolored red and purple, this deciduous shrub makes a sweet, graceful four-foot-tall accent, flowering summer and fall. If you are lucky you will find pink and white varieties, which show up even better in the shade. With enough water, hardy fuchsias will be happy in sunny locations too. A variegated species, Fuchsia versicolor, offers leaves marbled with gray and pink tones.

For fragrance in your shade garden, be sure to include summersweet (*Clethra alnifolia*). The flowers are white, and the new cultivars 'Pink Spire' and 'Rosea' are both light pink. Because their forms are relaxed and their flowers are subtle, both summersweet and hardy fuchsia are very compatible with perennials.

There is no shortage of evergreens for moist shade; an abundance of rhododendrons, andromedas (*Pieris*), camellias, and sarcococca are yours to choose from.

Entire books have been written on the genus *Rhododendron*, so I will simply offer a few of my favorites, based on their form and foliage more than their flowers. I love *Rhododendron yakusimanum*—its new leaves look as if they are dusted with powdered sugar at the top and coated with brown suede on the bottom. Pink buds open to pale pink flowers, which become white with age. The shrub is compact and attractive year-round. Because it's such a good plant for the garden, many named cultivars are available. Heart-shaped leaves and bell-shaped pink flowers make *Rhododendron williamsianum* a favorite small rhododendron for the shade. I also like the taller *Rhododendron daphnoides* for its dark-green lobed leaves and purple flowers.

Rhododendron 'Snow Lady' with fuzzy leaves, graceful white flowers and rounded form is lovely in all seasons. So many rhododendrons catch my eye in bloom time but bore me most of the year with drab green leaves and awkward woody branches that I am very careful to choose them primarily for form and foliage.

Andromedas (*Pieris japonica*) are fine spring-flowering shade-loving plants with small leaves and fragrant clusters of pendant white or pink flowers. Be sure to place them where their ultimate ten- to twelve- foot height is welcome. I placed one in front of the foundation of my first house and was surprised to see it get far taller than its alleged six feet. I moved to my second house to discover that the prior owner had played the same trick on me. After six years of living with it, the andromeda was finally farmed out to a friend who needed it for a screen, and now I can see out my kitchen window again.

Japanese camellias (*Camellia japonica*) can be a bit somber in the shade with their dark green leaves, but are hard to beat as tough tall hedges for backdrop screening. Their early flowers cheer the heart, but I confess to enjoying them from a distance, in other people's gardens, as their dying brown flowers bother me. I do love *Camellia* × *williamsii* with glossy dark green leaves and flowers that fall off before they turn brown, especially 'Mary Christian' with pink trumpets, and the semidouble dark pink 'Donation.'

> *If the browned blossoms of* Camellia japonica *remain obstinately on the bush they will generally yield to a smart tap on the branches with a stout walking stick or a hoe-handle.* . . . Camellia × williamsii *varieties are well mannered about this, and it will be found that all the species shed their flowers except when frosted.*
>
> —Lys de Bray
> *Manual of Old-Fashioned Shrubs*

Sweet box (*Sarcococca*) is one of the best shade-loving evergreens, with deep green, glossy, tapered leaves that look as if they've just been polished, and small white fragrant winter flowers. On a recent February day, walking in a friend's garden, I stood still suddenly, delighted with a sweet perfume. It was sweet box— its fragrance appeases my wintertime longing for the garden and hints that spring will be here soon. Three species of sweet box can beautify your damp shade garden: the low ground cover, *Sarcococca hookeriana humilis*, the three- to four-foot shrubby *Sarcococca confusa*, and the taller five-foot *Sarcococca ruscifolia*.

Damp shade supports a rich perennial palette. Hellebores thrive there with ample winter bloom. Beginning in late winter, lungwort with leaves of solid green (*Pulmonaria angustifolia*) or spotted white (*Pulmonaria saccharatta*) makes a low blue-flowering ground cover to accompany early daffodils. Ferns unfurling in spring add their lacy texture and cover up the dying leaves of the daffodils. Astilbes, with ferny leaves, offer plumy flowers blooming red, pink, white and cream in June. For contrast, hostas with bold rounded leaves contribute green, blue-green, and variegated patterns to the foliage tapestry. Their flower spikes are white or lavender, and several are prized for fragrance: 'Honey Bells,' 'Royal Standard,' and *Hosta plantaginea*. Majestic ligularias and rodgersias will flourish in shade as long as you're generous with water. Slugs come running as soon as the young leaves of hosta and ligularia emerge, so liquid slug bait is the first line of defense. Powder and pellet forms of slug bait can be fatal to pets.

My favorite ligularias are 'Desdemona,' with large, rounded burgundy leaves and stems, and 'The Rocket,' with deeply indented triangular leaves and spikes of yellow flowers. Equally dramatic, the majestic rodgersias are unsurpassable in damp shade. Their bold leaves command your attention while their plumy flowers have the same delicacy as astilbe. Shieldleaf rodgersia (*Rodgersia tabularis*) emerges from a brown knob at ground level, expanding to form bright green circular leaves two feet across, like water-lily pads. I fully expect to see elves peeping out from underneath these fantastic frisbees. The second surprise occurs when the flower spike shoots up, rising five feet tall on a narrow stem to flower in midsummer like a great cream-colored astilbe gone haywire. The flower stands tall and then tips to one side, leaning rakishly at the top like an ostrich plume.

Fingerleaf rodgersia (*Rodgersia aesculifolia*) has handsome leaves shaped like the horse chestnut tree, and creamy white flowers. Featherleaf rodgersia (*Rodgersia pinnata*) has bold pinnate leaves and creamy-pink flowers, while its select form 'Superba' has bronzy leaves and pinker flowers with a longer bloom period. An eye-catching combination at Great Dixter paired a blue-leaved hosta with featherleaf rodgersia. Add some burgundy astilbes and you'll have a rich color combination with good textural contrast—boldest rodgersia, medium-sized hosta leaves, and ferny foliaged astilbe.

The earliest, June-flowering astilbes are mainly arendsii hybrids, growing two feet tall in shades of white, cream, pink, peach, red, and even lavender. They look heavenly in drifts and combine well with ferns, hostas, Japanese primroses and masterwort (*Astrantia major*). At Butchart Gardens in Victoria, British Columbia, deep red, pink, and cream astilbes blend in the dappled shade of a lacy tree like an impressionist painting. Near the lake at Van Dusen Gardens in Vancouver, British Columbia, light pink, raspberry pink and red astilbes flower in shade, doubled by their reflections in the water. Nearby in sun, taller Japanese iris in shades of blue and purple enhance the astilbes.

Masterwort (*Astrantia major*) with its handsome dissected leaves thrives in moist shade, its lacy cream flowers blooming repeatedly summer and fall if you keep cutting off the spent flowers. If you get behind and let the spent flowers go to seed, you will be rewarded by seedlings that self-sow at the base of the mother plant.

To carry the color into late summer, try the short lavender-pink *Astilbe chinensis pumilla*, or the tall lavender-pink *Astilbe tacquetii superba*. Add the white spikes of bugbane (*Cimicifuga racemosa*) or ironweed (*Veronicastrum virginicum*) for a pink-and-white composition.

Some of the showiest shade lovers make dramatic appearances in spring only to yellow out and disappear by midsummer. Don't forgo these prima donnas; just make sure you have a supporting cast to follow up when they fizzle out. The spectacular bleeding heart (*Dicentra spectabile*) with heart-shaped pink and white flowers suspended from arching stems can be interplanted with astilbes or ferns that will carry through into summer. Columbines (*Aquilegia* hybrids) with elegant spurred flowers in shades of pink, yellow, blue, white and even maroon, can be grown in the early empty places beside hardy fuchsias that will fill in during summer and fall.

· SOME LIKE IT HOT ·

Where it's hot and sunny, you have two choices. Alter the environment by creating shade, or capitalize on the benefits. A hot sunny place is just right for a swimming pool, tennis court, or a garden of sun-loving, heat-tolerant plants. To find likely candidates for your garden, think about places in the Temperate Zone that are similar and consider the plants that flourish there: the Mediterranean countries, Australia, the southwestern and midwestern United States. Then compare hardiness zones and see whether your climate is a good match. Where the plants are too tender to be perennial in your garden, you may choose to grow them as annuals. I grow the heat-loving dahlias, zinnias, and cosmos originating in Mexico as annuals for extra color in hot places.

Plants that originate in mountainous regions with rocky soils that dry out in summer are good bets. Many tulips are native to Turkey, Greece and Iran, where hot, dry summers are the norm. The same is true for many of the flowering onions (*Allium*), grape hyacinth (*Muscari*), glory-of-the-snow (*Chionodoxa*) and crocus. A browse through *The Bulb Book* by Martyn Rix and Roger Phillips will show you just how the terrain looks with bulbs coloring

rocky inhospitable sites. Some plants flourish where others collapse. Our job is to understand what plants need and provide it,
making them and our gardens happier for the effort.

Many alpine plants have found ways to adapt to intense winter cold and wind followed by extreme summer heat and drought.
Some crouch in cushiony forms as if hugging themselves small and
low out of the wind's way. Others sprawl low and flat like mats.
Thrift (*Armeria maritima*), snow-in-summer (*Cerastium tomentosum*),
cottage pinks (*Dianthus plumarius*), rock cress (*Arabis caucasica*),
pussy toes (*Antennaria dioica*), and thymes are just a few examples of
these low-growing rock-garden plants. If we are careful to give
them the gravelly, lean, well-draining soil they are used to in their
usual habitat, they will grow happily in dry heat. These are excellent crevice plants for rock walls and stone patios in full sun.

Leaves that are gray, silver, hairy, woolly, waxy, leathery, or
narrow are all characteristic of plants doing their best to conserve
water and reflect sunlight. The smaller the leaf surface, the smaller the area from which leaves can lose water (transpire). Since
transpiration takes place from small openings (stomates) on the
underside of leaves, the smaller the leaf surface, the fewer the stomates and the less water that will be lost.

Thick, fleshy leaves are another way for plants to hold onto
water, so succulents and sedums with this trait will be good plants
for hot places. Deep roots that can seek water far beneath the surface and thick carroty taproots are also helpful adaptations to
drought. We are after the camels of the plant world. Like the
camel, some of these plants may not be as glamorous as their
moisture-loving cousins, but their adaptability to a challenging
situation makes them more attractive than less sturdy plants that
will wilt or burn.

For the front of the border or ground cover in hot places, look to the herbs for sturdy, aromatic plants: lavender, thyme, sage, artemisia, santolina, and rue. Purple-spiked 'Hidcote' lavender, pink-flowering 'Hidcote Pink,' lavender-colored 'Grosso' lavender are just a few of the fragrant possibilities to use as individual accents or low hedges to frame a flower bed. Creeping thymes flower white and shades of pink with green, gray-green, or golden foliage. I love creeping lemon thyme for its delightful lemon scent and early green and yellow foliage, and 'Clear Gold' thyme for its permanently yellow-green foliage. 'Clear Gold' thyme looks wonderful with clumps of red Japanese bloodgrass coming through it.

Purple sage is a favorite edging plant in my garden, combined with purple annual verbenas, pink 'Park Princess' dahlias, and a charming annual cerinthe from New Zealand with blue-green leaves and purple flowers. Golden sage is in good company with purple penstemon 'Midnight Blue' and yellow-flowering lady's mantle. Rue, with its blue-green leaves, can edge a border or hedge a bed. I love it in front of pink or peach miniature roses. Feathery gray 'Silver Mound' artemisia or filigreed *Artemisia canescens* are also attractive at the edge of a bed in front of 'Elfin Pink' penstemon. Grow these low artemisias as a ground cover or interplant bulbs between the crowns of the plants. The large whimsical globes of violet *Allium christophii*, flowering on short sturdy stems, make a jazzy combination with gray artemisia in June.

Gray santolina is happiest spilling down a wall or rock garden, with red miniature roses or orange-red sun roses (*Helianthemum* 'Henfield Brilliant') nearby. Another foamy draper, Mexican daisy (*Erigeron karvenskianus*), is a nonstop bloomer all summer and fall, with white daisies that turn pink. It's lovely with the larger flowers of pink evening primrose (*Oenethera speciosa*) and blue-green rue nearby.

To attract hummingbirds, try the California fuchsia plant (*Zauschneria californica*) that loves to drape down a sunny bank, and enhance it with *Euphorbia myrsinites*, a gray-leaved spurge that looks like a creeping eucalyptus and flowers bright yellow in winter. Or contrast the gray-leaved spurge with the darker succulent foliage of 'Vera Jameson' sedum, which flowers pink in late summer.

Choices abound in the three- to four-foot range for the dry sunny garden. Yarrows, with large platelike flowers, are showy in a wide color range. Try red 'Paprika' yarrow with yellow daylilies and light-yellow 'Moonbeam' coreopsis. 'Salmon Beauty' yarrow, a pastel peach color, is pretty behind gray-leaved lavender or blue-green rue, with spikes of blue longleaf speedwell (*Veronica longifolia*) nearby. Yellow 'Moonshine' yarrow with gray ferny foliage marries well with the blue balloon flowers (*Platycodon grandiflorus*). Plant three balloon flowers for every yarrow to keep them in balance: balloon flowers take longer to grow into substantial clumps.

It would be great fun to turn a big sunny space into an herbal meadow, using masses of yarrow in shades of yellow, peach, and lavender, billowing drifts of lavender, feathery green and bronze fennel for taller accents, a sea of yellow-flowering silvery curry plant (*Helichrysum angustifolium*), splashes of gray 'Powys Castle' artemisia, accents of gray-white 'Valerie Finnis' artemisia, and the orange butterfly weed (*Asclepias tuberosa*) to jazz up the color scheme. Imagine the fragrance of lavender and curry plant, all the silvery foliage of artemisia glistening in the hot sun and the colorful butterflies dancing from lavender to butterfly weed!

Daylilies are stalwart perennials that are easy to grow, long-lived and forgiving in full sun, hot, dry places, and even in partial shade. I look forward to the scent and grace of early yellow lemon lily (*Hemerocallis flava*), with its charming recurved petals. It makes its spring debut in a sea of blue meadow cranesbill (*Geranium pratense*) in my garden. 'Frank Hunter', a summer-blooming creamy light-yellow daylily, can flaunt its ruffled flowers behind a lower hedge of deep blue-violet 'Hidcote' lavender. Pink- and peach-tinted daylilies look equally showy with lavender, or beside steely blue sea holly (eryngium) and fall flowering 'Autumn Joy' sedum, with succulent foliage and pink blooms. The delicately colored 'Catherine Woodbury' is a favorite daylily for its pink-lavender flowers. Light-yellow 'Moonbeam' coreopsis in front of 'Catherine Woodbury' would echo her yellow throat.

In hot sun, *Gaura lindheimerii* is a must for continuous summer and fall flowering, drought tolerance, and charm. Although each flower spike is narrow, with pink-white blooms flowering from the bottom of the spike upward, the volume of stems on one plant is great. Stems wave about freely and weave through nearby speedwell and summer phlox. Let the rampant obedience plant (*Physostegia virginiana*) roam through a mass planting of gaura and send its three-foot pink flowers through in late summer, and add some 'Carmen' sedum for thick umbrellas of pink fall color.

Where it is sunny and moist, try the gaura with purple coneflower (*Echinacea purpurea*) for a long-lasting color combination. Add some oriental 'Casa Blanca' lilies for August scent and a bold white accent.

Jupiter's beard (*Centranthus ruber*), with its gray-green leaves and rosy-pink flowers will grow anywhere, even in rock walls, and flowers repeatedly during the summer. A weed elsewhere, in dry places it is a gift. The same is true for the peach-leaved bellflower (*Campanula persicifolia*) which flowers in blue spikes for most of the summer and seeds around the garden to appear in unexpected places. Its blue bells enhance the pink beards of centranthus, and daylilies in shades of yellow would brighten the picture further.

There are plenty of deciduous shrubs and shrubby perennials for dry sunny places. The tree mallow (*Lavatera thuringiaca*) forming a six-by-three shrub loaded with pink summer flowers is a good choice; its 'Barnsley Pink' form with pink-centered white flowers is even more striking. Butterfly bush, gray-leaved with white, pink, blue, or purple fragrant summer flowers, is a fine backdrop plant. Most roses will flourish in full sun, with the exception of hybrid musks, which prefer afternoon shade. In 1992, our hottest, driest summer to date, 'Red Coat' rose, with single red flowers, outdid itself. The deep pink Bourbon, 'Zephirine Drouhin' flowered profusely, and the sea tomato roses (*Rosa rugosa*) flowered well and set abundant hips. All of these roses are underplanted with hardy geraniums, lamb's ears, sage, and artemisia to anchor them to the ground and add foliage and flower color.

Where evergreen shrubs are needed in heat, I like the gray *Senecio greyii*, the khaki-gray Jerusalem sage (*Phlomis fruticosa*), and the gray-leaved rockroses (*Cistus*), although these last are only marginally hardy where I live. Of the three, Jerusalem sage, with bright yellow spring flowers, is the toughest. Sturdier yet, but unappealing to me, the brooms and junipers offer drought tolerance.

The strawberry tree (*Arbutus unedo*) is an unusual evergreen shrub that can grow to the size of a small tree. It has waxy green leaves, small white pendant flowers, and fruit reminiscent of strawberries. As it ages, its bark turns red-brown and craggy. Use it to make a handsome hedge or screen—it does very well in full sun with little water. So does glossy abelia (*Abelia grandiflora*), a large evergreen shrub flowering pinkish-white in late summer. Cotoneaster lacteus is another small-leaved evergreen beauty with arching branches covered with white flowers in spring and orange berries in fall.

A choice tree anywhere, the blue Spanish fir (*Abies pinsapo* 'Glauca') can take warm dry places. The stiff blue-green needles are arranged in a pleasing pattern that reminds me of a woven basket. Equally striking, blue Atlas cedar (*Cedrus atlantica* 'Glauca') is a good candidate for a specimen tree in a hot dry place. Some of the pines do well in heat, as do most of the crabapples and hawthorns. The golden rain tree (*Koelreuteria paniculata*) is a fine small tree with clusters of yellow flowers in spring followed by papery lanternlike seed pods. Its leaves look ferny and turn yellow in autumn.

· SLOPES ·

Steep slopes can be inhospitable places in the garden. Very few of us like to spend our gardening time climbing or crawling, let alone maneuvering wheelbarrows or tools, up and down slopes. The first steep bank I designed was a challenge, and not just from a design point of view. I am leery of heights, and my client was fearful of snakes that might be lurking in the tall grasses of this overgrown hill. We were quite a tense pair surveying the steeply pitched slope. It was hard to imagine the outcome, but in fact this forbidding site was to become a sensational flower garden within the year.

Acrophobia aside, slopes can be tamed and turned into useful garden spaces in a variety of ways. Historically, steep hillsides in Mediterranean countries have been terraced to create vineyards and olive groves. The handsome stone walls that support terraces enhance the beauty of the plants that are more easily grown and tended once the ground has been leveled. We can build terraced flower gardens using stone, concrete, or treated wood for the retaining walls, with steps to move from level to level. Please hire a very experienced landscape architect or stonemason before you undertake a project that involves reshaping the earth. Structural strength is critical when you are retaining masses of wet soil, and you need an expert. Team the builder with a horticulturist to make sure that the design of wall and terraces will be suitable for growing the plants you have in mind. Too narrow a terrace will limit the depth of your planting bed. Aesthetics, horticulture, and engineering all need to be considered to create a successful terraced garden. Keep the size and shape of the terrace walls and floors in good proportion to each other, and to your larger garden.

Take a trip to Powys Castle in Welshpool, Wales if you want to study a shining example of garden spaces. There a series of 500-foot-long terraces have been carved out of a large hill. Each terrace houses exquisite perennial borders framed by low boxwood hedges. The walls retaining these terraces shelter colorful shrubs and vines, many of which are marginally hardy and benefit from the walls' warmth and protection from the wind. It's hard to know where to look first: the flowering perennials command your attention as much or more than the enchanting view of distant woodlands beckoning from the opposite direction.

When you plan a terraced garden, consider your point of view. If you are looking down on the terraces from an upper level, choose plants that are attractive from above, for example the silk tree (*Albizzia julibrissin*) or the doublefile viburnum (*Viburnum tomentosum*). Both of these flower at the tops of their branches. An

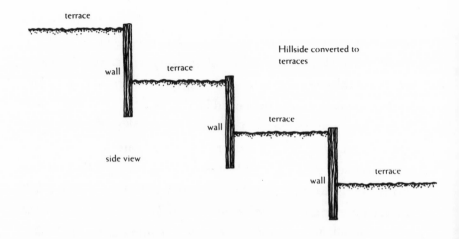

terrace

wall

terrace

wall

terrace

wall

terrace

side view

Hillside converted to
terraces

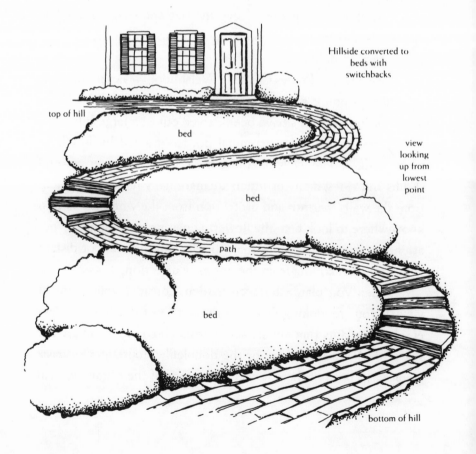

Hillside converted to
beds with
switchbacks

top of hill

bed

bed

view
looking
up from
lowest
point

path

bed

bottom of hill

aerial view lends itself to the formal shapes of a parterre (patterned garden)—for example, an herbal knot garden. When viewing from a distance, think about using broad sweeps of color by planting masses of the same plant in drifts, or shapes that are pleasing. The shapes of paths, stairs, and walls will contribute to the overall design and should have broad, bold lines, especially if seen from far away.

Switchbacks are an alternative way to ease the difficulties of gardening on slopes, just as on hiking trails. Beds can also be terraced in a modified way by building low retaining walls at their base, so that you can rake the soil at a more gradual pitch within the bed. Paths designed in a pattern of switchbacks can curve around the beds so that both gardener and visitor can get up and down the slope easily. These beds are actually island beds, with easy access for planting and grooming.

A northwest garden that I love, with a steep site overlooking a lake, employs this technique. The owners brought in tons of crushed rock to make switchback paths that swing around sizable oval and rectangular island beds. The site is in full sun, and the beds are crammed with shrub roses, herbs, and perennials in marvelous color combinations. Both sides of the garden are screened from neighboring properties by fences, which support climbing roses and clematis. The bed farthest from the house, at the lowest end of the slope, is used to grow favorite fruits and vegetables. You can peek over the fences to see what the neighbors have done to solve the problem of gardening on a steep site. Both have covered their banks with conventional ground covers: ivy and juniper. It is a study in contrast.

Ground covers are certainly an option in steep places, but

most gardeners who love color and texture will shudder to see so much potential gardening space devoted to one kind of plant. It's hard enough to have the discipline to plant three or five of one kind of plant—an entire hillside is just too much.

If, however, you truly have enough gardening space elsewhere, and simply want to cover a slope completely, here are some good ground covers for the job.

In sun, the evergreen bearberry cotoneaster (*Cotoneaster dammeri*) with small, glossy leaves, white spring flowers, and red fall berries is hard to surpass. Ground-hugging and attractive year-round, it spreads quickly enough without running amok. The taller, deciduous rock cotoneaster (*Cotoneaster horizontalis*), two feet tall and six across, has a herringbone branching pattern and red fall berries. Its variegated form has leaves edged with white that turn pinkish in fall.

Hardy cranesbills will serve well as ground covers in sun or shade. Try *Geranium macrorrhizum* where you need a low evergreen cover, and enjoy its magenta-pink flowers. For long summer color, *Geranium endressii* with bright pink flowers, spreads quickly, and the taller *Geranium* × *oxonianum* 'Claridge Druce' will travel faster and farther. Long-blooming blue-violet *Geranium ibericum* will cover well and quickly, too.

Although I find most junipers unappealing, I do like the shore juniper (*Juniperus conferta*) for its soft, bright green needles. Heaths (*Erica*) and heathers (*Calluna*) are a bit wispy looking to me, but they can be attractive massed on a bank, especially when they flower. A mixture of heaths and heathers will give you spring and summer color. Use groupings of each to have strong enough impact. Be sure to shear them after they bloom to keep them compact. To dress up a bank of heaths and heather, interplant drifts of spring bulbs and summer-flowering *Clematis viticella* hybrids. The bulbs will flower at the same time as the spring-flowering heaths, and the clematis will scramble over the heaths and heathers, flowering ahead of the heathers.

Bunchberry (*Cornus canadensis*) makes a lovely ground cover in shade, with oval leaves and white spring flowers that tell you it's a dogwood. It establishes slowly. Sweet woodruff covers quickly, with a carpet of fine-textured bright green leaves and fragrant white May flowers. Evergreen privet honeysuckle (*Lonicera pileata*), a low, spreading handsome shrubby plant with glossy leaves, does well in shade or sun. There are many more plants to choose from. I must confess that even on a steep bank I would do my best to make a flower garden, for that is what gives me the most pleasure.

Our terrifying snake-infested bank was converted by a landscape architect and a strong-backed crew to a series of terraced beds, with one central, steeply sloped rectangle that remained to be planted with perennials. Still descending a good forty-five degrees, it needed strong-rooted plants to hold the soil and big sweeps of color to be enjoyed from above and below. I chose summer- and fall-flowering perennials with long bloom periods to maximize the color. A sweep of light yellow 'Moonbeam' coreopsis defined the top edge of the bed, a mass of 'Autumn Joy' sedum with pink fall flowers held the lower edge, with an underplanting of blue dwarf fall asters. Sides of the bed were edged with gray santolina backed by red miniature roses on the left and gray lambs' ears backed by coral miniature roses on the right. The central part of the bed was filled with dozens of blue *Aster frikartii* and a drift of pink 'Pleasant Hill Pink' daylilies.

Color blazes on this bank from June to October. Only the miniature roses need faithful grooming to look pretty, and they are within easy reach at the sides of the beds. At the end of the season, all perennials are cut down nearly to the ground, and a top dressing of finished compost is applied. Low-maintenance perennials were chosen because gardening on a slope is challenging, and the fewer tasks required, the better.

A slope can also be turned into a rock garden and become home to the many alpine plants that grow in the mountains. Give the plants the same conditions they are used to in their native habitat, and they will thrive. For information about alpines and how to build rock gardens, read *Rock Gardening* by H. Lincoln Foster, and George Schenk's *How to Plan, Establish and Maintain Rock Gardens*. You will also benefit immensely by joining the American Rock Garden Society and its local chapter closest to you. A current edition of *Gardening by Mail* by Barbara Barton or your local botanic garden will have the society's most recent mailing address.

I saw the most beautiful conversion of a slope to a rock garden in England, naturally, in a garden called Eldswood. Because its banks are elevated, it is pleasing to view them from below, as if you were approaching a mountain. At Eldswood the view was framed from below: a weeping silver pear tree and a sumac were placed with just enough space between them to glimpse a small pond and a rock garden rising on a bank above the water. This early enticing view made me look forward to exploring the rock garden in all its details. A central staircase made of railroad ties and packed with earth made the ascent easy. Rocks and alpine plants were placed artfully to both sides of the steps with occasional gravel side paths into the rock garden to encourage exploring. Most of the plants were ground hugging, creeping, draping, and mounding, typical shapes found naturally in an alpine scree at the base of a mountain. Bright pink, vivid orange, vibrant yellow, and electric blue were used to good advantage for viewing from a distance, from both above and below the slope.

Creating a waterfall is a costly but dramatic treatment of a slope. This is often done in Japanese gardens and can be studied there and in nature. Proper placement of rocks for effective and convincing waterfalls requires an expert in this specialized garden art form. Take your time finding the right designer and visit his or her completed work to be sure you like the results. Interview past clients to be certain that the work was done well, and you will save yourself a great deal of trouble. I have found that the best way to find an expert is word of mouth. If you ask around and the same name is mentioned more than once, with good marks, you have probably found a competent designer. If you are new to an area, inquire at the closest quality nursery, horticulture department, or botanic garden to begin to get some leads.

· POOR SOIL ·

Where I live, the soil is so full of clay that you could use it to make pottery. Blue-gray in color, this earth is so slick and mucky that the first time I put a shovel in the ground, I could hardly get it out again. When I finally did manage to pull the shovel out, there was an ominous sucking sound, and my heart sank at the prospect of gardening in mud.

In the summer, this kind of soil turns to concrete. The cracks that form on the surface are large enough to drop a trowel down. A friend who visited the garden in its first summer still tells the story about the time she pulled a plant label out of the ground to read the plant's name. When she tried to put it back in the ground, the earth was so hard that the label snapped in half.

Oddly enough, almost all my students come to class with similar stories, and they all think that they alone have the worst soil. When we start comparing notes, there is great comfort in realizing that not one of us has perfect soil in the beginning. The complaints vary: too much clay, too much sand, too many rocks. We all start out with imbalanced soil, and our first job in the garden is soil improvement.

Most of us know what perfect soil looks and feels like. I first came across it at a friend's nursery, and my heart soared—it was like falling in love. I could put my hand into that soil halfway to my elbow; that's how lovely that earth was. It had been river bottom at one time. If you ever have a chance to buy land like this, grab it.

It is heavenly to dig, plant, and weed in a loose, crumbly soil that yields easily to shovel and trowel. Plants grow easily in friable earth, spreading their roots freely, just as you can wiggle your toes in beach sand. Water moves through loose soil, nourishing the plants and then draining down. The roots take in the water and air that they need without drowning in standing water.

The ideal soil has enough organic material in it to hold some moisture, yet drains freely. Whether we start with clay, rocks, or sand, we have to add the main ingredient for good dirt: compost. I have used gypsum, manure, and peat moss to improve the soil, but compost has proven to be the very best addition.

In a garden I helped to design and plant, we inadvertently performed a controlled experiment. With a limited budget, we had only enough money to improve half the border with compost. When the plants grew up that summer, the results were so clear they could have been used to advertise compost. The plants on the left side of the border, where compost had been added, were stocky and deep green; those on the right, where we ran out of compost, were puny yellow runts.

You can buy compost, or make your own. To find sources of compost, look in the Yellow Pages under "Bark," where you will find many listings. Call to compare ingredients and costs, and don't be shy about asking the vendor exactly what is in the mix.

Mushroom compost is the medium that was used to grow last year's mushroom crop. It starts out as a mixture of peat moss, ammonium nitrate, gypsum, pumice, wheat germ, straw, and manure, so it is rich in nutrients. Occasionally mushroom compost produces a crop of unwanted mushrooms in my garden. Some companies sell mushroom compost in its pure form, while others mix it half-and-half with garden mulch.

Garden mulch is recycled yard debris and is usually sold by a recycling company that charges you to dump your yard debris, then grinds it up, lets it age four to six months, and sells it back to you as garden mulch. Of course you can go into business for yourself by grinding up your own prunings in a chipper and letting them age. Or you can start composting without any machinery by sticking to the softer garden waste: leaves, grass clippings, vegetable peelings, eggshells, coffee grounds, annual weeds, and used potting soil.

Making your own compost is satisfying work: you are turning garbage into black gold. For the quickest results stick to the soft leaves, grass clippings, and kitchen debris and stay away from woody prunings. Make a pile up to four feet tall, and keep it damp. Turn the pile to hasten decomposition. If you're not in a hurry, let it rot on its own. A pile is just as good as a series of bins, but not as organized looking. A series of bins allows you to move the compost from one place to another efficiently and makes a tidier appearance.

With three bins, your first bin will have the beginning debris stacked several feet high. Turn it into the second bin after a while, let it rot some more, and then move it into the third bin, where it will break down to finished compost. You can sift it through a screen if you have time, and the final product will be uniformly fine-textured. You can make bins from wood, wood and wire mesh, concrete block, or chicken wire. Our metropolitan recycling organization has compost bins on display for the public to see. Your city may have a similar demonstration.

The simplest bin is a four-foot-tall cylinder of chicken wire. Drop all your soft debris into the top of the cylinder. Wait a few months, and the stuff will compress down to a foot or so. Lift the cylinder off the pile, turn the pile a time or two, and move your finished compost to the bed in the garden that needs it most.

One summer I played around with these simple chicken-wire bins. After tangling with a springy roll of chicken wire, I discovered that I could tame it by cutting the length of wire I needed off the roll with wire cutters, laying it on the ground, and weighting it down with concrete blocks for a day to take the bounce out of it. Then it was easy to shape the sheet of chicken wire into a cylinder, stand it upright, pull all the cut wires on one end of the mesh through the grid on the other end, and bend the cut wires back to fasten the cylinder shut. I made three cylinders four feet tall and two feet across and hid them behind some five-foot-tall blueberry bushes. In late summer I filled them with leaves, windfall apples, and grass clippings. The following spring, I had a foot of coarse compost at the bottom. I lifted the wire cylinders up and forked the compost over to the nearby blueberry bushes, which have benefited from the nutritious mulch.

If you have a big garden as I do, you will probably have too much debris to fit into bins. I have found it easier to make huge piles right where I need new beds and let them turn into compost over the course of a year.

I built raised beds in my garden by following garden designer Liz Marantz's example. She lays layers of overlapping newspapers several sheets thick on the ground to kill the grass. Then she piles grass clippings, leaves, annual weeds, and kitchen waste several feet high and waits. A year or so later, she has a raised bed ready for planting, with the resulting compost now compacted down to a foot or so high.

When I first began gardening, I spent a lot of time and energy adding compost to the existing soil, spading it in, raking and smoothing it to a blended soil. No matter how much compost I added to my heavy clay soil, it was never enough. One year necessity taught me a lesson. I had ordered a large number of Siberian iris which arrived in fall, and much to my dismay I had no bed space left to plant them. A new bed was needed—pronto. Desperate, I decided to cheat. I bought a large quantity of compost, piled it up three feet high, and shaped it into a circle. Voilà—I had an instant raised bed for my iris. The plants settled into that lovely compost and thrived.

That was my first experiment in improving the soil by building a raised bed. It was such a success that I do it routinely now. Every summer and fall I pile leaves and grass clippings four feet high wherever I want to break ground for next year's beds. By the following spring, the pile has turned into compost that I plant in.

Last year I took another shortcut that will help you if your garden is big. I had a three-year-old compost pile that was twenty feet long and four feet tall at the very back of my property. Exhausted by the thought of trying to move all that soil where I wanted it, I decided to hire a retired farmer to help me. He drove into my garden on a small tractor with a front-end loader. With his cowboy hat and Western boots, he was like the Lone Ranger coming to the rescue. I told him where I wanted the compost moved and added some hand signals when it got too noisy to talk. He roared around on his tractor, shoveling great scoops of compost with his front-end loader until he had moved and shaped it into a long, marvelously tidy berm. In one hour he moved that huge mass of earth with great panache and ease; my back was spared hours of agonizing work. Although there can be a great sense of accomplishment in doing things yourself, there are times like this to hire help and appreciate the value of machinery in the garden.

· CONTAINED RAISED BEDS ·

You can push the principle of raised beds a little further to create *contained* raised beds. These are simply raised beds framed by low walls of stone, brick, or weather-resistant wood. I have seen them used for vegetables and cut flowers, and it struck me that they are actually very big planter boxes without bottoms. Their advantages are many: you can fill them with rich soil; the raised level cuts down on back strain; and the soil warms up sooner. The frames or walls can be made wide enough to serve as low ledges to sit on. The hard surfaces of wood, brick, or stone also add structure to the garden and can be softened by draping or billowing plants.

In a garden I helped with, the owners were tired of mowing a large sloping backyard that descended to wilderness with no clear demarcation. They had the sloping ground raised with retaining walls to create a level surface, got rid of all the grass, and made a floor of crushed rock. Then they built several curved raised beds by stacking flat, thick rocks two to three feet high and filling the space within with rich soil. This allows them to enjoy flower and vegetable gardening without strenuous bending, and they eliminated mowing the grass.

In a Mercer Island, Washington, garden that I visited, an ingenious landscape architect conquered a hillside by building a series of large bottomless planter boxes in pleasing rectangular shapes. The boxes gave structure to the space and broke the hillside into smaller, manageable planting beds. Roses and herbs bloomed happily on the hot sunny slope in rich soil that had been brought in to fill the constructed boxes.

Ten

Container

Gardens

Gardening in containers is great fun. You can control the soil, the drainage, experiment with color to your heart's content, and change the composition with ease. Flowers are closer to eye level, so you can see them better and enjoy their fragrance more.

Small plants that are lost in a big border are better enjoyed in pots, where they are in scale with the smaller picture. Draping

plants that sprawl onto the lawn only to be shredded by the mower can be used well at the edge of pots where they spill gracefully
over the rim. This is a good lesson to follow in the garden: instead
of getting unruly plants to behave, find a place where they can be
happily rambunctious.

In a wet climate, since pots are up above ground level, the
plants have a fighting chance against slugs. The few unwanted
visitors are easy to find and remove: they always lurk at the pot's
rim, where it is cool and moist, or underneath the pot.

Because pots are substantial and hard surfaced, they can
serve as focal points in a bed, along a path, to mark an entry, or to
signify a new space in the garden. Like sculpture, they are solid
enough to be good anchors where the garden is ethereal and
needs grounding.

Even an empty container can serve this purpose if its shape is
graceful. A terra-cotta urn placed at the end of a colorful walkway
gives the eye a resting place and indicates the end of a composition, just like the blank space at the end of a chapter. You pause
there before turning the page.

Containers bring color to places that need seasonal cheer:
on the porch, patio, deck, and around swimming pools. They
greet the visitor with ebullience like a warm welcoming commit-
tee. Because it's so easy to fill them with rich potting soil, pack
them with plants and fertilize them often, their flowers perform
even better than those in the ground.

To have successful containers, think big. Dinky little pots
will dry out fast and look skimpy. A large, deep container with
drainage holes at the bottom will give you the space to grow an
abundance of plants for a rich combination of colors and textures.

I love big bowl-shaped pots made of glazed ceramic, in dark

or muted colors, that set off the flowers without distracting from them. Grayed blue, dark green, charcoal are some colors I prefer. Warm-colored terra-cotta containers are also lovely but do tend to chip and get mossy. A friend coats hers with water sealer and says this prevents chipping. Plastic versions of terra-cotta are sturdier and cleaner, but go against my grain. I like garden ornaments to be related in color and texture to nature's bark, stone, earth, and greens.

Although tubs and barrels made of redwood, cedar, and oak are serviceable as planters, they don't please me visually. I do love urns made of metal, cast iron, bronze, or copper that has been aged to a patina. To me, stone and concrete planters usually look too massive and cold for residential gardens.

I've seen some whimsical containers made from recycled materials, and I encourage you to use your imagination. An old tin coal bucket, clay flues, drainage tiles standing on end, an old birdbath, stone watering troughs, ancient wheelbarrows, and elderly carts are just a few of the possibilities. Old enough to be leaky, they will give your plants drainage and add a touch of charm to the garden.

Because plant roots can spread only so far inside a container, it's very important to fill the container with rich potting soil. Avoid dry woody mixes that look like bark dust—feel the soil you are buying and make sure that it is moist, dark, and crumbly. Imagine that you are a plant and ask yourself whether you'd like to spread your roots in this soil. Don't be afraid to ask to feel the potting soil if it's already bagged: a conscientious merchant who wants your repeated business will show you a sample.

Make sure your container has drainage holes before you plant in it, or your plants will rot. You can fill the bottom of a very deep container with Styrofoam peanuts to keep the weight down. Then top it with a foot or two of potting soil, enough to allow the roots to spread. To leave room enough for the plants, fill the container about a foot shy of the rim. You can sprinkle granules of slow-release fertilizer on the surface of the soil, then unpot your plants and arrange them on the surface. Finally, fill any gaps between them with more potting soil, smooth and tamp the soil to eliminate any air pockets, and water thoroughly with a hose-end watering wand until you can see water draining out the bottom of the container.

Nothing is more important than consistent watering for healthy, colorful containers. Skimpy or erratic watering will stunt your plants. They will stop growing when they are dry. Touch the surface of the soil in your pots to test for dryness; when it feels dry, water thoroughly. Depending on the temperature and wind, you may need to water daily. Hanging pots in summer's heat may need watering twice daily. Think of how thirsty you get in summer's scorching heat and then imagine that you're a plant and can't walk to the sink. Have compassion for your container plants, and they will reward you with nonstop color. Make it easy on yourself by placing your pots close to a water supply.

Annuals bloom for so many months that they need a steady diet of fertilizer, especially in containers with water constantly washing through. I like to start the season with a balanced liquid fertilizer numbered 15–30–15. The first number tells you the percentage of nitrogen, which helps leaves to grow; the middle number indicates the percentage of phosphorus, which encourages bloom production; the last number states the percentage of potash, important in seed production.

When the plants have grown and are flowering well, I switch

to a liquid fertilizer that concentrates on promoting blooms, usually numbered 0–10–10. Equally important, I remove all spent flowers to prevent the plants from going to seed. Once annuals start forming seed, they stop flowering, so it's up to us to deadhead regularly.

My favorite containers are bowl shaped, three to four feet across and two to three feet tall. This size gives me enough room to plant some tall focal plants at the center, some lower billowy plants around them, and some draping plants to spill over the pot's rim, for a lush, vibrant picture.

I believe in the stuff-and-cram method of planting pots; my goal is wall-to-wall color. For quickest shows of color, I like to use the biggest, fullest plants I can find: gallon-sized perennials, four-inch pots of annuals, the largest bulbs available. After all, the growing season is always too short, and we want our color *now*. Unlike trees, where we plan for the future size and shape, container gardening lets us be impulsive and indulge ourselves for the immediate season.

Since annuals grow best with a minimum of root disturbance, I stay away from those grown in crowded tray packs. Separating the young seedlings inevitably tears their roots. Then they sulk for so long that you lose a week or two of growing time. I like to use four-inch pots or six-cell packs; in both cases, the plants can be popped out and replanted without shocking the tender roots and continue to grow smoothly.

You can get several seasons of color from the same container if you are willing to plan ahead. I love early color in the garden, so I plant bulbs and early annuals for spring interest. When they finish flowering, I remove them and replant the pots with annuals, perennials, and bulbs for summer and fall. In late summer, I sometimes replace any shabby-looking annuals with fall perennials to refresh the color.

Containers can be used singly or in groups. One large pot can serve as a focal point within a larger bed. A single urn of lily-of-the-Nile (*Agapanthus*), with its impressive globes of blue flowers on stout stems, has strength enough to stand alone.

I think about pots the same way that I look at island beds, as small, colorful worlds unto themselves. Like island beds, they often look better in groups that relate to each other, unified by a common color scheme or by repeated use of the same plants.

Sometimes I place several containers together on one level, and sometimes I stage them so that some are taller than others. Wide stairways are great places for staging pots. Even better are stairs that lead nowhere. I have a set of stairs leading to a back garage door that never gets used. This is a fine place to play with containers, and the dark blue door makes a great backdrop for bamboo and ornamental grass that I can grow safely in containers without fear of turning them loose in the flower beds.

I also create many layers of color by mixing hanging baskets, window boxes, and pots at ground level. This method is effective near porches and patios. Sometimes in a dull bed, where the season's color is spent, I use an old-fashioned wrought-iron plant stand with tiers of outreaching arms. I fill it with trailing geraniums, pink 'Sofie' or beet-red 'Harvard,' and draping white-and-purple 'Whirligig' African daisy (*Osteospermum*). By midsummer the plant stand has disappeared behind a tapestry of flowers cascading to the ground.

I dream of someday hanging dozens of moss baskets from the overhead grid of my grape arbor, to color up the shady space below the grapevines. I'll fill them with upright and trailing fuchsias with pink and purple flowers, pink and magenta impatiens, blue and white browallia, and trailing blue lobelia. Then I'll take a blanket and sit under the grape arbor, enjoying the color.

In planting a large container, I like to have one or several center plants to serve as the main focus, surrounded by a skirt of shorter plants and a final tier of draping plants. Here are some of my favorite combinations:

For spring, I like a centerpiece of about twenty-five tulips, blending shades of light pink, dark pink, and burgundy that bloom at the same time. I'm partial to the mid-spring flowering 'Triumph' tulips in containers for their moderate height; I especially like the cup-shaped forms such as hot-pink 'Attila' and pastel-pink 'Douglas Baader.' I surround these tulips with the slightly shorter 'Cheerfulness' daffodils that also bloom in mid-spring. Their double flowers are thick and rich looking, white with a touch of yellow at the center. At the edge of the pot I like the dark 'Blue Jacket' hyacinths, which bloom ahead of the tulips and daffodils and contribute early fragrance. I tuck blue pansies and 'Pink Charm' rock cress between the hyacinths for added color, if there is enough room.

I love the luminous 'Apricot Beauty' tulips surrounded by white 'Thalia' daffodils. 'Thalia's' long, tapered petals flare outward like wings; the flowers look poised for flight. Sky-blue 'Roy Davidson' lungwort (*Pulmonaria*), light-blue pansies, or iridescent 'Delft Blue' hyacinths make a fine finishing touch at the edge of the pot.

For a spring display, all of these bulbs must be planted the previous fall. Pots must be weatherproof to winter over outdoors, with walls thick enough to withstand freezing and cracking. Less sturdy pots can be sheltered in cold frames or on a protected porch or cool daylight basement, with enough watering to keep them moist. Cool-weather annuals can be tucked in when spring arrives, perennials added in fall or spring.

For summer displays, I first remove all the bulbs and cool-weather annuals. If time allows, I plant the bulbs in drifts elsewhere in the garden, but I admit that often in the spring rush they end up on the compost pile. Last spring I did have a very fragrant and colorful compost border. All the hyacinths and tulips from the previous summer pushed through the pile and flowered away. A lovely surprise.

Before I add the summer annuals, I sprinkle more slow-release fertilizer on the soil. Then I pack in as many plants as possible. Here are some colorful combinations for full sun:

I love to use princess flower (*Tibouchina urvilleana*) for a centerpiece. It's a woody annual that looks like a miniature tree and grows four feet tall and more, depending on summer's heat and the pot size. This exotic Brazillian plant has red-edged velvety green oval leaves and spectacular three-inch-wide bright purple flowers. I nag nurserymen to grow this plant, for I *must* have it. I surround it with pink African daisy (*Osteospermum* hybrids) that branches out, reaching toward the edges of the pot, with showy flowers blooming at the ends of strong stems. I tuck in a few vanilla-scented purple heliotrope between the African daisies, and for a finishing touch, plant lavender-blue Swan River daisies (*Brachyome iberidifolia*) and 'Silver Brocade' artemisia close to the pot's edge. Hundreds of small blue daisies froth over the rim, creating delicate blue lace beside the bold gray leaves of the artemisia.

When the pots are large enough, I like to add occasional pink accents by using 'Elfin Pink' penstemon and deep burgundy 'Garnet' penstemon to spice up the color. The fragrant dark red-brown chocolate cosmos (*Cosmos atrosanguinia*) makes an exceptionally nice novelty addition.

I repeat similar pink, blue, and gray combinations nearby in smaller pots using annual 'Blues' geranium, which is actually pink, with blue Swan River daisy and gray lotus vine. The shorter geranium is more in scale with a smaller pot, and the lotus vine repeats the gray of 'Silver Brocade' artemisia in a more delicate texture.

In shade, my favorite plants for centerpieces are the upright annual fuchsias, which flower abundantly if watered and fertilized faithfully. I love 'Gartenmeister Bonstedt' fuchsia. Its brilliant tubular coral flowers sparkle against the rich dark green and maroon leaves. 'Salmon' impatiens makes a fine skirt for the fuchsia, with flowers of the same hue yet a contrasting round shape. A trailing edge of pale chartreuse 'Limelight' helichrysum completes the unusual trio. A striking composition by designer Jane A. Smiley joined 'Gartenmeister Bondstedt' fuchsia and maroon coleus, with coral splashes in the coleus's leaf, echoing the color of the fuchsia's flowers.

In partial shade, I love tall 'June Bride' fuchsia with its countless tubular, bright pink flowers, along with shorter purple-and-red 'Lord Byron' fuchsia. I add white annual browallia for its clean, star-shaped flowers and blue Swan River daisies or blue 'Sapphire' trailing lobelia to drape over the rim.

There is always that place far away from the water faucet that needs a pot. Where survival depends on drought tolerance, try the sedums, sempervivums, and herbs. You can create a tapestry of red, green and gray-green by mixing the hens and chickens (sempervivums) with sedums in different foliage colors. Add some golden sage for contrast and some 'Lemon Gem' marigolds with lemon-scented foliage and tiny yellow flowers. Or try geraniums with rose- and lemon-scented leaves and surround them with draping rosemary or billowing silver thyme for contrast.

Even the prettiest pots begin to look frazzled in August. Re-assess the plants and remove any that are over the hill. Replace them with fall-flowering chrysanthemums and late-summer-blooming window-box dahlias. I like to pot up the peacock flow-ers (*Acidanthera bicolor*) for filling the late-summer gaps in beds and pots. These are tender bulbs that I plant in spring, five or so to a gallon container. In July I slide them carefully out of the contain-er and replant them where I need extra color. Their maroon-cen-tered white flowers are striking and just the right height (15"–20") for a container, or at the front of a border.

· WINDOW BOXES ·

Window boxes add charm to the exterior of a house and bring the flowers closer to eye level from inside the house. Paint them the same color as the house if you want them to blend in; stain or paint them a contrasting color for more drama. Walking around an English village early one morning, I was delighted to see the many wooden window boxes filled with maroon, yellow, and blue pansies, all with faces at eye level for close-up enjoyment, with lace curtains in the windows behind them.

You can dress up your home with copper window boxes or, better yet, copper aged to a verdigris. For spring, plant dwarf daf-fodils for close-up early color: white 'Jenny,' yellow 'Tête-à-Tête,' dainty yellow 'Hawera' and fragrant yellow 'Baby Moon' are some favorites. Brighten the picture with single, early foot-tall dark-red 'Couleur Cardinal' tulips. Tuck in some rich purple-blue netted iris (*Iris reticulata*) and blue pansies. Let the double white rock cress (*Arabis albida* 'Florepleno') drape over the edges.

One spring day, driving down Northwest 23rd Street in

Portland, I spotted a window box so lovely that I had to stop the car. A symphony of pinks, wines, whites, and pale yellows greeted me. On closer inspection, I saw poor man's orchid (*Schizanthus wisetonensis*) with glorious flower clusters in shades of pink, rose, coral, white, lavender, violet, maroon, and yellow. This is a cool-weather annual that is a perfect foil for bulbs and needs a container or window box for proper enjoyment of its detailed flower patterns and delicate ferny leaves. Fragrant stock, with thick flower spikes in shades of purple, reddish-purple, and lavender, added vertical strength to the planting. Double-white 'Cheerfulness' daffodils, early pink tulips, light-pink and light-yellow primroses, and pastel-pink pansies with maroon centers completed the rich picture. The scents and colors filled me with joy.

Receiving this gift of beauty on an ordinary spring day reminded me of how much gardeners give to others and themselves. I used to think that gardening was a rather selfish occupation because I love it so much for my own pleasure. When I stop to enjoy a window box, I understand that we all gain from each other's beautiful creations, and I know that art and beauty are as important to a full life as food and water. Contributing beauty is a form of healing as important as finding the cure for disease.

> *It is clear to me that the main purpose of a man's life is to give others what is in him. Such a matter is not a question of selfishness or unselfishness. Mozart was probably rather selfish in a childish way, but he gave the world what was in him, and what a gift! We only have what we are, and we only have what we give.*
>
> —George Sarton

Eleven

While Your Garden Is Growing Up

If you space your trees and shrubs with enough room to develop over time, you are faced with staring at bare ground for many years. To avoid dullness and boredom, you can fill the empty places with fast-growing perennials and annuals. As your permanent plants mature, you will have to remove your fillers, little by little, and transplant them or share them with friends. Moving

193

and dividing plants can also become the beginning of a small nursery, if you choose.

Here are some of the easygoing filler plants that I have used over the years to break new ground and fill developing beds. Hardy geraniums (cranesbills) are versatile enough to grow in sun or shade, damp or dry soil. The low-growing bloody cranesbill (*Geranium sanguineum*) has vibrant magenta-pink flowers and small divided leaves; it spreads quickly to cover the ground. Its pastel-pink cousin, *Geranium sanguineum* 'Striatum,' is a little more restrained and equally beautiful. A bit taller and spreading faster, *Geranium endressii*, with its bright pink flowers, will cover large, empty spaces in one season and flower all summer. Its color is a bit intense for me, and I find 'A. T. Johnson,' with creamier pink flowers, easier to blend with the pink and deep-red shrub roses that I grow nearby.

Hardy geraniums in shades of blue and blue-violet are marvelous peacemakers. They marry well with the pinks and reds of peonies and old roses that flower beside them in June and help quiet the warring screams of red-orange poppies and pinkish-red peonies that insist on flowering at the same time. In shade they can serve as a unifying carpet beneath rainbow plantings of pink, red, and creamy yellow rhododendrons or multicolored plantings of azaleas.

A marvelous combination in a sunny Seattle garden joined the pink alba rose 'Celestial' with McKanna hybrid columbines in shades of blue, pink and yellow, with blue-violet *Geranium ibericum* at ground level anchoring the composition and uniting the colors. *Geranium ibericum* is about a foot and a half tall and two feet across, with beautiful lobed leaves. Very similar in appearance, *Geranium himalayense* has more daintily divided leaves and blue-violet flowers. I like it near lady's mantle (*Alchemilla mollis*), flowering at the

same time with sprays of delicate yellow-green flowers. Lady's
mantle can be a pest, but it's a useful pest, filling in the gaps in sun
or shade, spreading by roots and by seed.

I like the three-foot-tall *Geranium pratense* for filling spaces in
my big mixed border. It flowers blue-violet at the same time as the
oriental poppies, peonies, and Siberian iris bloom. *Geranium
pratense* was a great help when the border was new. Six years later,
I am digging it out selectively where the plants have grown up.

The white and yellow loosestrifes are quick fillers and not
too difficult to dig out when they have served their purpose. The
plants are about three feet tall, and their flower spikes cut well for
bouquets. The two yellow loosestrifes—*Lysimachia ciliata* and *Lysimachia punctata*—run readily underground and flower in late
spring. Spurned as weeds, these plants are good ground breakers
in big gardens. A choice cultivar, *Lysimachia ciliata* 'Purpurea' has
dark burgundy leaves to boot. White loosestrife (*Lysimachia clethroides*), also called goose-goes-walking and gooseneck loosestrife,
flowers in midsummer with whimsical arching flower spikes that
live up to its name. These plants run rapidly underground, especially in rich, moist soil, but that has never been a problem for me
since everyone wants a division.

Summer-flowering feverfew (*Chrysanthemum parthenium*) is a
great garden filler with small white blooms that cut well and harmonize easily with other colors. I am partial to the double white
form and love the pungent scent of its bright green leaves.

Love-in-a-mist (*Nigella*) is also called devil-in-the-bush. Ro-
mantic- or villainous-sounding depending on which name you
use, it's a lovely annual that seeds around freely. Intriguing blue
flowers, surrounded by a haze of ferny green leaves, turn to papery seed pods that can be dried for arrangements. If you leave

the seed pods on the plant, they explode eventually, bombarding the flower beds with shiny black seeds that germinate rapidly. Nigella is a great help at the base of leggy roses and between new shrubs. It does sometimes threaten to take over the garden, but I still prefer it to the creeping buttercups and dandelions that I'd have in its place. The same is true for the blue forget-me-nots that help cover the ground between drifts of springtime tulips and contribute to the compost pile when I weed them out in summer.

For some height in the early summer garden, I must have foxgloves (*Digitalis*) even though they, too, are overenthusiastic. I love their tall spikes of white and lavender flowers filling in between the roses and bellflowers (*Campanula*). They're easy enough to pull out when they get too thick, and there's always enough seed left in the ground for next year's crop.

I confess to a love-hate relationship with the tall, summer-flowering annual *Verbena bonariensis*, the verbena from Argentina. Its five-foot-tall, branched stems produce a myriad of small purple flowers that attract the butterflies. The flowers bloom from summer until frost. However, each flower seeds down prolifically and I can never deadhead in time. I love the flowers, and I hate the monumental amount of weeding required to keep this annual in bounds. Weigh the pleasure against the pain before you allow this plant into your garden.

Annual cosmos and spider flower (*Cleome hassleriana*) also self-sow from year to year and are marvelous fillers where you need five feet of height. They are only moderately aggressive in spreading and are very useful for color in new gardens. Cosmos are available in several shades of pink and white. I find the orange form less vigorous, at least in our relatively cool Pacific Northwest summers.

Cleome offers pink, violet, and white flowers and returns

from seed faithfully from year to year. With all of these self-seeders, the main caution is to familiarize yourself with the leaf shape of your seedlings so that you don't inadvertently weed them all out with the dandelions. When in doubt about a weed, wait a little while. It may turn out to be a choice seedling.

Flowering tobacco (*Nicotiana*) will return from seed and fill gaps in a border, especially the old-fashioned three-foot-tall fragrant strains that scent the garden toward evening. The exotic white annual jasmine tobacco (*Nicotiana alata*) and the woodland tobacco (*Nicotiana sylvestris*) are both unusual species that can be grown from seed for summer drama and evening perfume. I like the newer dwarf hybrids in red, pink, and lime-green for fillers in developing beds because the flowers are small enough to blend nicely with existing shrubs and perennials. I especially enjoy the pale-yellow 'Lemon Starship' nicotiana and the 'Lime Green' variety.

Although I love zinnias and dahlias for their bright showy flowers, I find them more difficult to mix with perennials and shrubs because of their stiffer branching and bolder flowers. It's like trying to wear a Japanese kimono with a Mexican hat.

I find most marigolds too stumpy and bright to integrate in a bed or border. When I first started gardening, I loved their ease of germination and found it very satisfying to deadhead marigolds, for they snap off with a crisp sound, like a cap gun. The tiny signet marigolds (*Tagetes tenuifolia*) are the kind I love now, with ferny leaves and an abundance of tiny flowers that bloom in a cloud. Try the charming red 'Paprika' or lemon-scented 'Lemon Gem' with yellow flowers to fill some of the front-of-the-border gaps. These add zippy color without being garish.

Sample Plans

and

Thumbnail

Sketches

It pains me to see how many gardens are monotonous collections of broadleaf evergreens and conifers. So many people are uncomfortable looking at empty space, bare branches, and less-than-perfect garden pictures. Human nature seems to crave sameness, fullness, and perfection. We fear and resist change. We see the garden as an extension of our home and want to have it look furnished and finished. Please leave that kind of perfection to the interior designers and allow room in the garden for change, surprise, and unfolding.

Remember how each of us changes and evolves in the course of a lifetime—and yes, it's mysterious and sometimes even disturbing. But it's the nature of life on earth.

And Lucy, now, was thirty. When she looked at herself in the mirror she saw the faint imprint of another face imposed upon the familiar contours of her own. She observed this…with a certain perplexity; it was as though you cohabited with a mysterious stranger, and conducted a subdued and secret struggle for house-room. . . . What would one turn into?

—Penelope Lively
Cleopatra's Sister

We want things the same, and yet excitement in our lives and in the garden comes through change. At thirty I had a predictable conventional job; at forty I designed gardens and lived by the seat of my pants; at fifty I write about gardens. Who could have predicted this metamorphosis?

Leave room for some surprises in your garden. Winter sticks become summer roses. Empty winter spaces allow peonies and irises to unfold in the spring. Unless there is room for change, your garden will be dull. Take some risks, live a little dangerously, and you will have a garden full of life.

Scale ⅛" = 1'

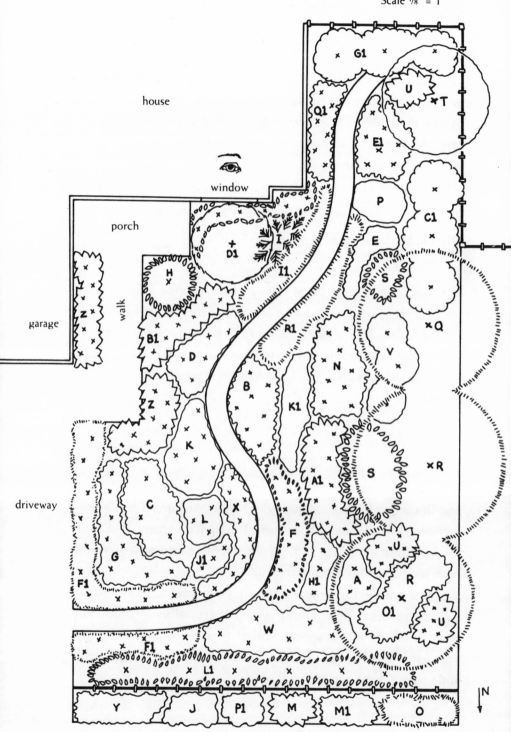

house

window

porch

walk

garage

driveway

G1

Q1

U
×T

E1
×

P

C1
×

E

S

Q
×

D1
+

I

I1

H
×

B1
+

Z

Z

D

B

R1

N
×

V

K1

K

C

L

J1

X

A1

S

×R

G

F1

F

U

H1

A

R

O1

U

W

F1

L1

Y   J   P1   M   M1   O

N

Entry garden with cottage garden look

L	E	G	E	N	D
A	Aconitum carmichaelii		A1	Helleborus foetidus and 25
B	Anemone sylvestris			Daffodils
C	Aster frikartii		B1	Helleborus niger
D	Astrantia major		C1	Hydrangea arborescens or
E	Azaleas			'Annabelle'
F	Campanula carpatica		D1	Japanese laceleaf maple
G	Coreopsis 'Moonbeam'		E1	Japanese Anemone
H	Daphne 'Carol Mackie'		F1	Lavender 'Hidcote'
I	Deer fern		G1	Peegee hydrangea
J	Dianthus 'Bath's Pink'		H1	Phlox 'Alpha'
K	Echinacea purpurea		I1	Pink Astilbe
L	Echinacea 'White Swan'		J1	Platycodon grandiflorus
M	English viola		K1	Pulmonaria
N	Epimedium rubrum and 25		L1	Roses
	Daffodils			'Angel Face'
O	Erigeron karvinskiansus			'Ballerina'
P	Ex* Andromeda			'Bonica'
Q	Ex Fir			'Escapade'
R	Ex Pine			'Mary Rose'
S	Ex Rhododendron			'Nearly Wild'
T	Ex Tree		M1	Salvia superba
U	Foxgloves		N1	Sarcococca hookeriana
V	Fuschia magellanica (pink)'			humilis
W	Gaura lindheimerii		O1	Sweet woodruff
X	Geranium sanguineum 'Striatum'		P1	Veronica 'Crater Lake Blue'
Y	Helianthemum 'St. Mary's'		Q1	White Japanese Anemone
Z	Helleborus orientalis		R1	White Astilbe

*Ex = "Existing"

· A MAINLY SHADY ENTRY WITH ·
A COTTAGE-GARDEN LOOK

A contemporary home with a prominent window facing the entry garden had been landscaped with lawn, pine trees, azaleas, and privets. The owner, who liked colorful flowers, was understandably bored stiff and asked me to design a cottage garden. Fortunately, both she and her husband were ready to eliminate the lawn and most of the shrubs in favor of flowering perennials with long blooming periods.

This space is only 40' wide and 50' long, with a wide driveway to one side and a number of large pines to the other side. Because the pines screen the neighboring house, they remain, even though they darken the garden. A mass planting of evergreen privet planted between the house and the road was removed. A few existing rhododendrons beneath the pines remain to serve as understory for the trees and backdrop for the perennials. A few azaleas previously sitting in front of the picture window were moved to serve as skirting for hydrangeas. One existing andromeda was kept for an evergreen accent.

The site is mainly shady near the house, with some morning sun, and sunnier out toward the road. With the house so close to the road, the owners wanted picket fencing to give a sense of separation from traffic. This choice led to placing roses on the inside of the fence, so that their canes could lean and drape over it. Low-growing perennials soften the front of the fence, spilling out onto the road. This feature set the cottage-garden mood for this entry.

The owners prefer pink, blue, purple, white, and yellow. To give unity to the planting of roses, we stayed with shades of pink and lavender-pink, but chose single and double roses, with a combination of floribunda, shrub, hybrid musk, and David Austin roses for variety. Perennials draping in front of the fence were mainly in groups of six, and colors were mainly white, blue, and purple to contrast with the pink roses.

To break up the rectangular shape of the space and add a way through for strolling and gardening, I wove a long, broad S-curved path through the length of the garden. Where possible, I placed the same or similar plants on either side of the path so that the path winds through the middle of the garden instead of breaking it into two separate spaces.

The owners chose a laceleaf Japanese maple for place of honor in front of the picture window. To keep this architectural small tree dominant, subtle low-growing evergreen shrubs and perennials were selected to accompany it—dwarf sweet box (*Sarcococca bookeriana bumilis*), deer fern, and Christmas rose (*Helleborus niger*). These low evergreens offer plenty of winter color and fragrance without blocking the view out the window.

Farther away from the porch, we ventured into herbaceous perennials that would leave the dreaded empty spaces in winter. With evergreens by the doorway, conifers and broadleaf evergreens to the side of the property, the owners felt happy enough to allow room for summer and fall color to get the cottage-garden look that they wanted.

I chose herbaceous perennials with long blooming periods and fragrance, in shades of pink, blue, purple, yellow, and white. Two low hedges of fragrant, purple 'Hidcote' lavender framed the lower end of the path and part of the driveway. Blue-violet *Aster frikartii*, rose-pink and white coneflowers (*Echinacea purpurea*), and blue balloon flowers (*Platycodon grandiflorus*) with yellow 'Moonbeam' coreopsis billow out of the sunniest part of the bed near the driveway. A mass of lacy *Gaura lindbeimerrii* backs the pink roses.

In shadier places, white hydrangeas act as the backbone. Drifts of pink-and-white fall-flowering Japanese windflower (*Anemone japonica*) and spring-flowering foxgloves contribute height. Lower-growing pink-and-white astilbes, white masterwort (*Astrantia major*), and pink hardy fuchsias provide plenty of summer

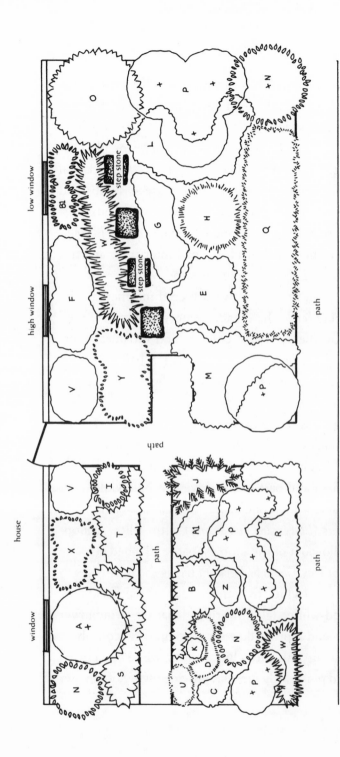

house

window

high window   low window

path

path

path

road   Low maintenance plan, east facing entry on a busy street   N

L E G E N D

A	Acer palmatum 'Sangokako'		H	Cornus alba 'Elegantissima'
B	Ajuga 'Burgundy Glow'		I	Daphne 'Carol Mackie'
C	Alchemilla alpina		J	Deer fern
D	Astilbe		K	Dicentra spectabile
E	Blue Aster frikartii		L	Epimedium ground cover
F	Choisya ternata		M	Evergreen candytuff ground cover
G	Coreopsis 'Moonbeam'		N	Ex* Camellia

O	Ex Pieris japonica		V	Nandina domestica
P	Ex Vine maple		W	Pacific coast hybrid Iris
Q	Ex Yew hedge		X	Sarcococca confusa
R	Geranium sanguineum 'Striatum' ground Cover		Y	Sarcococca hookeriana humilis
S	Hellebonus corsicus		Z	Solomon's seal
T	Hellebonus orientalis		A1	Sweet woodruff
U	Heuchera 'Palace Purple'		B1	Vaccinium ovatum

*Ex = "Existing"

color. Carpets of pink bishop's hat (*Epimedium* × *rubrum*), blue lung-wort (*Pulmonaria angustifolia*), white sweet woodruff and blue bell-flowers (*Campanula carpatica*) cover the ground instead of barkdust.

· A LOW-MAINTENANCE PLAN FOR · AN EAST ENTRY ON A BUSY STREET

This garden had its "bones" in place when I arrived to help put some icing on the cake. Because the house faced a busy road, the owners hired a landscape contractor to plant large shrubs and small trees for screening. Eleven vine maples (*Acer circinatum*) and a yew hedge stood close to the road as a visual screen and noise barrier. A large evergreen camellia and a mature evergreen an-dromeda stood at either side of the foundation bed, guarding the house. One path let directly from the street-side sidewalk to the front door. Another path split the left-hand rectangular bed in half, while the right-hand rectangular bed was interrupted with a series of concrete stepping-stones.

The owners wanted a blend of evergreen and deciduous shrubs, with perennials to add seasonal color. Since both owners work, they wanted low-maintenance plants. The desired look was natural woodland, low-key and informal, with occasional color accents.

Two immediate needs seemed obvious: a strong focal point against the house to be enjoyed from the main entry path, and an equally beautiful specimen against the dark yew hedge, for view-ing from inside the house.

We chose the red-stemmed 'Sangokaku' Japanese maple to show off against the house. In winter its red branches would stand out; in fall its yellow foliage would light up the garden. Against the yew hedge, red winter stems of variegated Tatarian dogwood (*Cornus alba* 'Elegantissima') add color and repeat the maple's red branches. The dogwood's white flowers and green-and-white leaves brighten up the somber yew in spring and summer.

Two evergreen heavenly bamboos (*Nandina domestica*) on either side of the entry patio were chosen for vertical emphasis and red fall color. Groups of the taller sweet box (*Sarcococca confusa*) and dwarf sweet box (*Sarcococca bookeriana humilis*) contribute evergreen foliage and winter fragrance to the shady entry. Two Mexican orange (*Choisya ternata*) placed beneath the tall window embellish the wall and add fragrant spring flowers. A 'Carol Mackie' daphne planted near the door wafts delicious spring scent. Winter-flowering hellebores and spring-flowering grassy Pacific coast hybrid iris skirt the taller shrubs.

Closer to the road, ground covers add flowers and foliage color. In the left-hand bed, accents of burgundy 'Palace Purple' coral bells, showy pink bleeding heart, white Solomon's seal, and astilbe rise up from their surrounding ground covers of 'Burgundy Glow' bugleweed (ajuga), sweet woodruff, and deer fern. In the right-hand bed, low spring-flowering evergreen candytuft and bishop's hat (epimedium) spread beneath the groves of vine maple, and a group of blue *Aster frikartii* combined with a drift of yellow 'Moonbeam' coreopsis make a central splash of summer color.

· A SUNNY ENTRY WITH · YEAR-ROUND COLOR

This small south-facing courtyard measures a scant 15' square. A 17' × 5' bed extends to the left of this courtyard, in front of the garage, making the complete entry garden into a backward L.

When I arrived, the courtyard had been paved with brick in the shape of two crosses, and the owners wanted to work around this existing pattern. The ground itself was a blank slate.

In such a small space, symmetrical plantings strengthen, simplify, and unify the design. The owners wanted two small trees on opposite sides of the path, no taller than ten feet. Rather than work hard to keep trees from getting out of hand, we decided to plant two shrubs of the 'Dawn' viburnum that had been trained to single trunks. This would give us the appearance of trees, yet stay the size of shrubs, in good scale with the small space. 'Dawn' viburnum blooms in fall and winter with fragrant pink flowers, a sensational feature for a place with daily foot traffic. The shrubs were surrounded by spring-flowering, white carpets of evergreen dwarf candytuft (*Iberis sempervirens* 'Little Gem').

A fragrant evergreen winter daphne (*Daphne odora*) that blooms in February grows sheltered beside the door, and the scented evergreen clematis (*Clematis armandii*) is trained over the entry—it blooms white in April. Hedges of fragrant purple 'Hidcote' lavender bloom to either side of the porch in summer. Closer to the front sidewalk, framing the path, an edging of gray-leaved cottage pinks (*Dianthus plumarius*) greets the visitor with fragrant pink flowers in May. Symmetrical groups of *Aster frikartii*, purple coneflower, and gaura bloom in summer behind the cottage pinks.

Off to the right side of the central courtyard, pink 'New Dawn' rose and purple Jackman's clematis are trained to climb a low fence together, with gray 'Powys Castle' artemisia feathering out at the base, keeping the clematis roots cool and hiding the rose's awkward legs. Peonies and Siberian iris offer flowers for spring with mallow, phlox, bellflower, gaura, coneflower, and aster for summer.

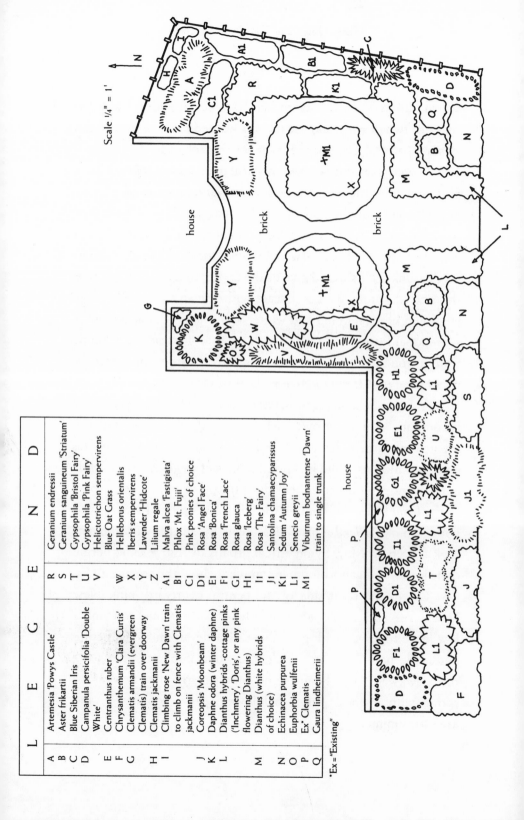

L E G E N D

A — Artemesia 'Powys Castle'
B — Aster frikartii
C — Blue Siberian Iris
D — Campanula persicifolia 'Double White'
E — Centranthus ruber
F — Chrysanthemum 'Clara Curtis'
G — Clematis armandii (evergreen Clematis) train over doorway
H — Clematis jackmanii
I — Climbing rose 'New Dawn' train to climb on fence with Clematis jackmanii
J — Coreopsis 'Moonbeam'
K — Daphne odora (winter daphne)
L — Dianthus hybrids -cottage pinks ('Inchmery', 'Doris', or any pink flowering Dianthus)
M — Dianthus (white hybrids of choice)
N — Echinacea purpurea
O — Euphorbia wulfenii
P — Ex' Clematis
Q — Gaura lindheimerii

R — Geranium endressii
S — Geranium sanguineum 'Striatum'
T — Gypsophila 'Bristol Fairy'
U — Gypsophila 'Pink Fairy'
V — Helictotrichon sempervirens
W — Helleborus orientalis
X — Iberis sempervirens
Y — Lavender 'Hidcote'
Z — Lilium regale
A1 — Malva alcea 'Fastigiata'
B1 — Phlox 'Mt. Fujii'
C1 — Pink peonies of choice
D1 — Rosa 'Angel Face'
E1 — Rosa 'Bonica'
F1 — Rosa 'French Lace'
G1 — Rosa glauca
H1 — Rosa 'Iceberg'
I1 — Rosa 'The Fairy'
J1 — Santolina chamaecyparissus
K1 — Sedum 'Autumn Joy'
L1 — Senecio greyii
M1 — Viburnum bodnantense 'Dawn' train to single trunk

*Ex="Existing"

Scale 1/4" = 1'

N

The left-hand narrow bed in front of the garage keeps the pink, blue, white and gray scheme going. Six roses bloom against the wall, several gray-leaved *Senecio greyii* hold the middle ground, with baby's breath and gaura making a lace of white and pink flowers against the roses. A few low-growing perennials in shades of pink and yellow spill out onto the sidewalk.

· GARDENS FOR CHILDREN ·

Given half a chance, most children will take an interest in the garden. After all, the garden is full of adventure for a naturally curious young person. The excitement of color, fragrance, fresh food, birds, butterflies, bees, and beetles abound. Opportunity to construct a bench, path, or fort attracts the budding builder. And then there is the miraculous process of growing a green plant from a small brown seed. A round, hard bulb goes in the ground in the fall, and up comes a tulip in the spring.

For children there is no limit. The garden becomes a place to cut flowers for arrangements, gather petals for potpourri, find the shiny hard-backed beetles, spot a nest full of baby birds, discover how a rose hip tastes. From children I've learned to sip the nectar from honeysuckle flowers, notice the frogs in my pond, and take the cats for reluctant rides in the wheelbarrow. This last adventure is largely an idea: the cats hop out well before the wheelbarrow is in motion. But it's fun to try.

And fun is the main spirit of gardening with children. My young friends who come to garden with me like to visit, chat, ask a million questions, touch and sniff the plants. Tasting is important, too: a leaf of licoricy sweet cicely, a strand of pungent garlic chives, some raspberries, a not-quite-ripe plum followed by a sour face.

Sometimes we weed together or pot up plants, but not for too long. Short periods of concentrated activity are enough—then it is time to check out the pond to see what insects are skating on it. So much is happening in the garden, and you wouldn't want to miss anything! Are the grapes ripe yet? Maybe next week. It's all so new for children that very little is overlooked.

When I ask friends how their children got interested in gardens, I get many answers. One mother of a five-year-old told me that her child, at three, showed such an interest in flowers that she herself began to notice them. They began gardening together. Sometimes it's a grandparent who takes the time to show a curious youngster how to sow peas. Teachers can open the door by showing children how to sow seeds on the classroom windowsill. Small events can make strong impressions.

Older children thrive on having their own gardening space where they can be the boss. A ten-year-old friend invited me to see his garden with great pride. In a small space, he had created a wonderful world of his own, complete with a path, a small bench, and a tapestry of lush plantings. Some of the plants were small starts from my garden, and it was amazing to see how they'd grown into big drifts.

We all enjoy the chance to play and experiment in the garden without anyone breathing down our necks, and children need the same sense of freedom. A small space that is all theirs can give them the empty canvas for creative gardening.

Plants that bear tasty fruit and vegetables are popular with children: blueberries, raspberries, cherry tomatoes, carrots, sugar-snap peas, parsley, and chives. Plants that mushroom overnight such as pumpkins, zucchini, and sunflowers are also very satisfying. Big bright flowers in primary colors are exciting: nasturtiums, tulips, marigolds, zinnias, cornflowers, bearded iris, shirley poppies, ladybug poppies.

Furry leaves are fun to touch: lamb's ears and *Salvia argentea* invite small fingers to pet them. Scented geraniums, lemon verbena, lemon thyme, Corsican mint, rosemary, lavender, and pineapple sage beg to be touched and pinched to release aromas. And of course chocolate cosmos, purple heliotrope, and evening-scented flowering tobacco (*Nicotiana*) are big hits for fragrance.

Give children their own garden, and you will be amazed at how they will grow. The garden allows all of us to share in the wonder of growing plants, observing the natural world, and having a taste of accomplishment in trying to orchestrate nature.

· AN EVENING-FRAGRANCE GARDEN ·

So many of us work all day. By the time we get home to enjoy our gardens, evening has arrived. Why not create a garden room with that in mind, concentrating on qualities we can appreciate from evening into nighttime. Sitting places are important; to gather and talk, relax, or reflect on the day's events. A water feature to catch the moon's light, and perhaps a jet of water for tranquilizing sound make an evening garden refreshing. Select plenty of white flowers that show up well at night, and include lots of fragrant plants for evening scents.

The sample evening garden has three places to sit: a patio for dining, with easy access to the house, a gazebo with built-in benches, and a small arbor with a built-in glider. All three seating places look out toward a central focal point intended to create a mood of restfulness. A small pond with a jet of water provides reflection and soothing sound. A narrow bed shaped like a cres-

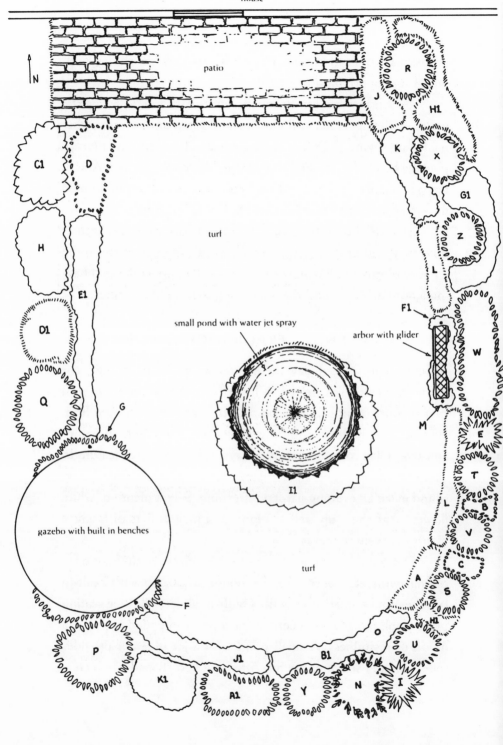

An evening fragrance garden

L	E G	E	N D
A	Artemesia pontica	U	Rosa 'Danae'
B	Blue Campanula persicifolia	V	Rosa 'Iceberg'
C	Campanula lactiflora	W	Rosa 'Lavender Lassie'
D	Campanula carpatica 'Alba'	X	Rosa 'Moonlight'
E	Casa Blanca Lily	Y	Rosa 'Nevada' (white)
F	Climbing Rose 'Iceberg'	Z	Rosa 'Prosperity'
G	Climbing Rose 'Sombreuil'	A1	Rosa 'Zephirine Drouhin' (pink)
H	Echinacea purpurea 'White	B1	Campanula Carpatica
	Swan'	C1	Senecio greyii
I	Gold Band Lily	D1	Silver Artemesia 'Powys Castle'
J	Gray santolina	E1	Sweet William
K	Lamb's Ears	F1	White Clematis 'Silver Moon'
L	Lavender hedge	G1	White Cleome
M	Ipomoea alba 'Moon Flower'	H1	White Cosmos
N	Philadelphus with Clematis recta	I1	White fragrant crescent moon
O	Geranium sanguineum 'Striatum'		bed with Nicotiana sylvestris
P	Rosa 'Gertrude Jekyll'		underplanted with White
Q	Rosa 'Heritage'		Sweet Alyssum
R	Rosa 'Autumn Delight'	J1	White Geranium sanguineum
S	Rosa 'Claire Rose'		'Album'
T	Rosa 'Class Act'	K1	White Phlox 'World Peace'

cent moon frames the pond on one side. It is filled with fragrant white *Nicotiana sylvestris*, underplanted with low, fragrant white sweet alyssum. The pond is surrounded by a carpet of grass, and flower beds full of roses and perennials embellish the perimeters of the space. Most of the roses are white, selected to glow at night; a few are pink and light yellow to avoid monotony. Almost all are fragrant.

Perennials, too, are predominantly white, with a few blue, pink, and lavender accents. Gray and silver foliage adds luminescence to the evening garden: lamb's ears, lavender, several kinds of artemisia, *Senecio greyii*, and gray santolina.

Fragrant lilies are tucked in between the roses: 'Casa Blanca' with glorious stems of huge white flowers, and gold-band lily (*Lilium auratum*) with yellow stripes on opulent white blooms. Laven-

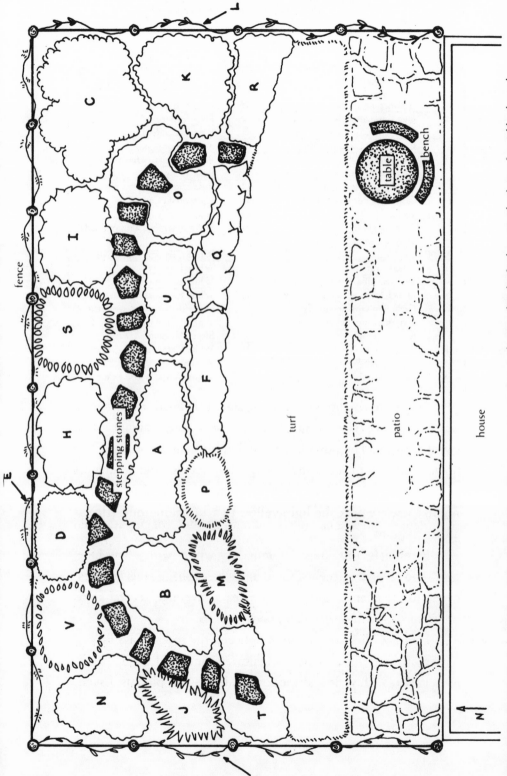

A sunny border for hummingbirds in a fenced back yard

L	E	G	E	N	D
A	Aquilegia formosa interplanted with 9 Crocosmia 'Lucifer'		K	Lobelia cardinalis	
B	Aster frikartii		L	Lonicera 'Dropmore Scarlet' train on fence	
C	Blue Michaelmas Daisy		M	Penstemon 'Ruby King'	
D	Buddleia davidii 'Empire Blue'		N	Phlox paniculata 'Starfire'	
E	Campsis radicans (Trumpet Creeper) train on fence		O	Phygelius 'African Queen'	
F	Coreopsis 'Moonbeam'		P	Pineapple Sage	
G	Eccremocarpus scaber (Chilean Glory Vine) train on fence		Q	Red Annual Nicotiana	
H	Hibiscus syriacus 'Bluebird'		R	Red Sweet William	
I	Hibiscus moscheutos		S	Ribes sanguineum	
J	Lily 'Enchantment'		T	Salvia superba 'May Night'	
			U	Veronica 'Sunny Border Blue'	
			V	Weigela florida	

der wafts its perfume into the night air along with sweet william and 'World Peace' summer phlox.

· A GARDEN FOR HUMMINGBIRDS ·

My first sight of a hummingbird visiting my garden was an exciting experience. Back then I grew plants for the love of color, and the hummingbirds were a bonus. Now I love the hummingbirds so much that I grow plants to attract them.

What's so special about hummingbirds? Maybe it's their small size and speedy maneuvers as they blitz the garden in search of nectar and insects. I like the way they first alert me to their presence with rapid, high-pitched chirps. The iridescence of their plumage and the way they can hover, whirring their wings at high speeds, delights me. I never tire of their air shows.

It's easy to draw them to the garden. They like spiders, whiteflies, and aphids, and heaven knows most of us have more than enough of these sources of protein. They need nectar, too, and head for the bright orange and red tube-shaped flowers in search of beverages.

In my garden the hummingbirds have appropriated an old dense hawthorn tree as their headquarters. This gives them a good launching platform for swooping forays on the sunny flower borders that I have planted thoughtfully with 'Lucifer' crocosmia, loaded with irresistible red tubular flowers in July. For later in the season, the more common orange crocosmia (*Crocosmia* × *crocosmiiflora*) flowers in August with funnel-shaped flowers that say "Drink me."

I wouldn't like a garden entirely orange and red, so the sunny border that I visualize for hummingbirds has touches of blue, purple, and yellow to balance the color scheme. Spring-flowering weigela, flowering currant, Formosan columbine and sweet william are included in the design to produce early supplies of nectar. The rest of the plants are summer- and fall-bloomers. To get the maximum amount of color, I've mixed shrubs, vines, perennials, and annuals.

Fences on three sides are mainly an excuse for training orange and red summer-flowering vines for the hummingbirds: perennial trumpet creeper (*Campsis radicans*) with showy orange flowers, 'Dropmore Scarlet' honeysuckle and red-orange Chilean glory vine (*Eccremocarpus scaber*). Staple plastic netting to the fence to make an easy trellis.

Red and orange flowers in the border will bring hummingbirds closer to the seating area, if you sit quietly. Orange 'Enchantment' lilies and purple 'May Night' salvia flower in June. July brings red-pink 'Starfire' summer phlox and blue *Aster frikartii*, red 'Lucifer' crocosmia next to 'Sunny Border' blue speedwell (*Veronica*) and orange-red 'African Queen' phygelius. 'Ruby King' penstemon and pineapple sage offer red summer flowers along with annual red nicotiana. A bit of yellow 'Moonbeam' coreopsis is added for color contrast.

The red tubular flowers and maroon leaves make the cardinal flower (*Lobelia fulgens*) exciting to us and the hummingbirds. Its August flowers extend the season, together with the blue Michaelmas daisies behind it. 'Empire Blue' butterfly bush (buddleia) and 'Blue Bird' rose of Sharon (*Hibiscus syriaca*) flower summer and fall, along with the dramatic large-flowered rose mallow (*Hibiscus moscheutos*).

· AN ENCLOSED MEDITATION GARDEN ·

This fenced garden room is intended as a private retreat. Open the gate, and a simple bench invites you to sit in front of a grove of five Japanese maples. Deer and autumn ferns unfurl their cooling fronds to both sides of the bench.

The floor of this space is crushed rock, plain and simple. A yin-yang symbol is the focal point across from the bench, planted with 'Silver Mound' artemisia and black mondo grass (*Ophiopogon planiscapus* 'Nigrescens'). Behind the yin-yang symbol, a multitrunked dancing peacock maple (*Acer japonicum* 'Aconitifolium') fills the northwest corner. Beneath it a planting of pink astilbe mixed with blue columbine extends to the gate. A small drift of ferny pink Jacob's ladder (*Polemonium carneum*) blooms to the right side of the maple, with linear blue oat grass (*Helictotrichon sempervirens*) for contrast. A tall group of plume poppy (*Macleaya*) shows off its bold blue-green leaves against the fence beside a clump of 'White Swirl' Siberian iris. Black bamboo planted in a sunken container makes a strong upright specimen in the northeast corner.

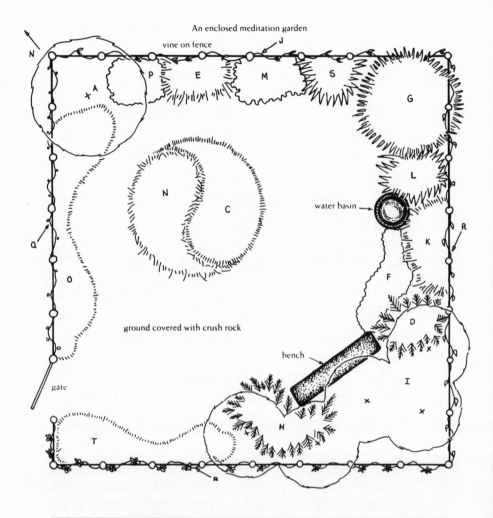

An enclosed meditation garden

	L E G E N D		
A	Acer japonicum 'Aconitifolium'	L	Japanese Iris 'Caprician Butterfly'
B	Akebia quinata vine on fence	M	Macleaya cordata
C	Artemesia 'Silver Mound'	N	Ophipogon planiscapus
D	Autumn fern		nigrescens Black Grass
E	Blue oat grass	O	Pink Astilbe and Blue
F	Carpet of lemon thyme		Columbine
G	Contained clump black bamboo	P	Polemonium carneum
H	Deer fern	Q	Porcelain berry vine Amelopsis
I	Grove of Japanese maple		brevipedunculata
J	Honeysuckle vine on fence -	R	Sasanqua camellia vine on fence
	Lonicera periclymenum 'Serotina'	S	Siberian Iris 'White Swirl'
K	Japanese blood grass	T	White Astilbe

Closer to the bench, a drift of 'Caprician Butterfly' Japanese iris displays white flowers with purple centers and veins. A small ceramic water basin forms a reflective accent in front of the iris. Four clumps of Japanese bloodgrass (*Imperata cylindrica* 'Rubra') make an interesting red-and-green foliage accent, with a carpet of lemon thyme at their base.

Fences act as framework for four vines with seasonal interest. The north fence is covered with shade-loving, evergreen *Akebia quinata*, bearing purple flowers. Evergreen sasanqua camellia adorns the east fence with shiny leaves and fall flowers. Porcelain berry vine (*Amelopsis*) displays its unusual iridescent turquoise berries in fall on the west fence. On the south fence, fragrant late Dutch honeysuckle (*Lonicera periclymenum* 'Serotina') flowers in summer.

To keep the mood quiet, color is subdued to foliage, and cool colors—blue, white, and pink—are dominant. The emphasis is on subtlety and simplicity, with enough detail to provide interest. The rustle of bamboo, grass, and iris leaves and the light fragrance of honeysuckle add to the pleasure of this garden.

· A CLOSING NOTE ·

I have led you down many garden paths, some real and some imagined. Each speaks its own beauty. When the gardener's heart is allied with nature, when the gardener's eyes and hands work in a loving way, a unique place will be fashioned. And not only will the ground be altered, and a garden unfold, but a new way of looking and knowing will occur. As much as the gardener affects the emerging garden, the process of gardening deepens the soul of the gardener.

Suggested Reading

. . .

Austin, David. *The Heritage of the Rose.* Woodbridge, N.J.: Antique Collector's Club, 1988.

Barton, Barbara J. *Gardening by Mail.* Boston: Houghton Mifflin, 1990.

Beales, Peter. *Classic Roses.* New York: Holt, Rinehart & Winston, 1985.

————. *Twentieth-Century Roses.* London: Collins Harvill, 1988.

Bloom, Alan. *Perennials for Your Garden:* Floraprint, 1981.

Brookes, John. *The Garden Book.* New York: Crown Publishers, 1984.

Capek, Karel. *The Gardener's Year.* Madison: University of Wisconsin Press, 1984.

Church, Thomas D. *Gardens are for People.* New York: McGraw-Hill, 1983.

De Bray, Lys. *Manual of Old-fashioned Shrubs.* Somerset: Oxford Illustrated Press, 1986.

Fish, Margery. *A Flower for Every Day.* London: Faber and Faber, 1964.

————. *Gardening in the Shade.* London: Faber and Faber, 1965.

Harper, Pamela. *Designing with Perennials.* New York: Macmillan, 1991.

Harper, Pamela and McGourty, Frederick. *Perennials: How to Select, Grow and Enjoy.* Los Angeles: Price Stern Sloan, Inc., 1985.

Hobhouse, Penelope. *Borders.* New York: Harper & Row, 1989.

————. *Color in Your Garden.* Boston: Little, Brown, 1985.

Lloyd, Christopher. *The Mixed Border* (A Wisley Handbook). London: Cassell Ltd, 1986.

————. *The Well-chosen Garden.* New York: Harper & Row, 1984.

Keen, Mary. *The Garden Border Book.* Deer Park, N.Y.: Capability's Books, 1987.

Lacy, Allen. *The Garden in Autumn.* NY: The Atlantic Monthly Press, 1990.

Paul, Anthony and Rees, Yvonne. *Designing with Trees.* Topsfield, MA: Salem House Publishers, 1989.

Proctor, Rob. *Annuals.* New York: HarperCollins, 1991.

Rix, Martyn and Phillips, Roger. *The Bulb Book.* London: Pan Books Ltd., 1983.

Sackville-West, Vita. *Garden Book*. New York: Atheneum, 1983.

Thomas, Graham Stuart. *Ornamental Shrubs, Climbers and Bamboos*. Portland, Oregon: Timber Press, 1992.

———. *Perrenial Garden Plants*. London: J. M. Dent, 1982.

———. *Shrub Roses of Today*. London: J. M. Dent, 1982.

Van Pelt Wilson, Helen. *Own Garden and Landscape Book*. New York: Weathervane Books, 1973.

Verey, Rosemary. *The Art of Planting*. Boston: Little, Brown & Co., 1990.

———. *The Garden in Winter*. Boston: Little, Brown & Co., 1988.

Weber, Belva. *How to Plan Your Own Home Landscape*. Indianapolis: Bobbs-Merrill, 1976.

Index

. . . .